9.7

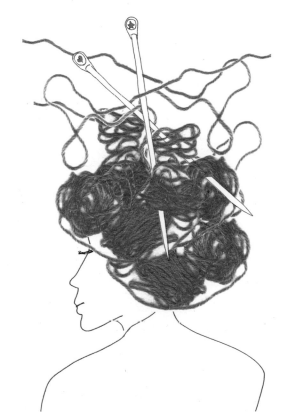

downtownDIY

Knitting

ALICE CHADWICK

with PAULINE HORNSBY

downtownDIY
Knitting

13 Easy designs for City Girls with Style

Watson–Guptill Publications / New York

Contents

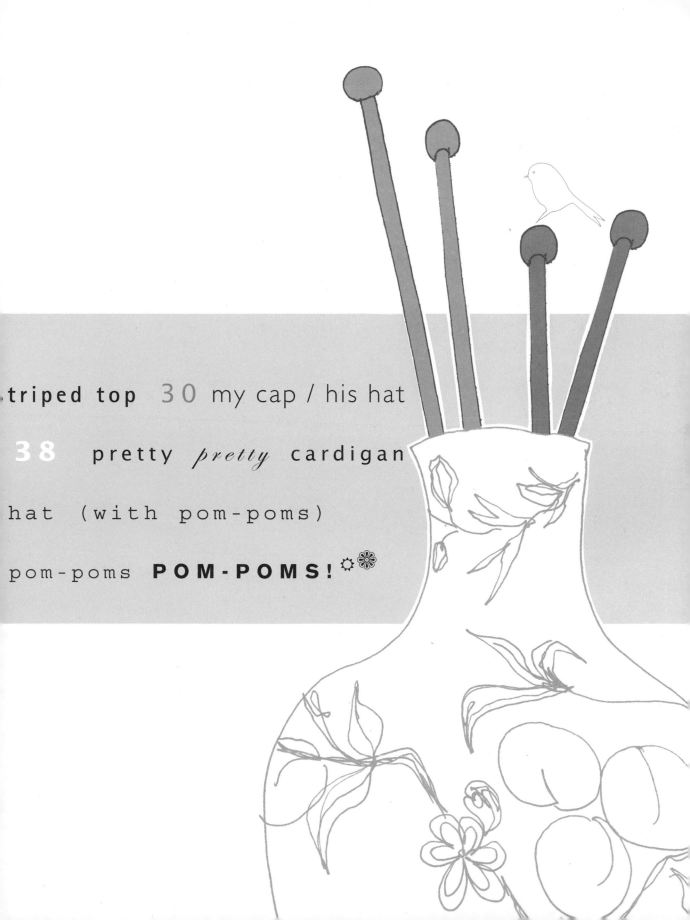

downtownDIY
Knitting

Tools

The essential tools for hand knitting are knitting needles and yarn. Needles come in a range of lengths, thicknesses, and materials, including metal, plastic, wood, bamboo, and casein. There are single-point straight needles for working back and forth, double-pointed needles for working in the round, and circular needles, which can be used with both knitting methods. The size of the needle used depends on the thickness of the yarn, the stitch pattern, and the effect you want to create.

metal straight
needles

scissors, tapestry needles, &
a tape measure are also essential

double-pointed needles

bamboo straight
needles

circular
needles

Here are a few more useful tools:

stitch markers are useful when knitting in the round to mark the position of shapings, stitch pattern changes, or a given number of rows or stitches;

stitch holders hold stitches not being worked while knitting continues on another part of the row;

straight pins are used when measuring gauge, blocking (see page 18), and sewing seams together;

crochet hooks are useful for picking up dropped stitches. Sometimes a knit piece is given a crochet border or button loop;

row counters are used to keep track of how many rows you've knitted.

s t i t c h   m a r k e r s

c r o c h e t
h o o k

s t r a i g h t
p i n s

s t i t c h
h o l d e r

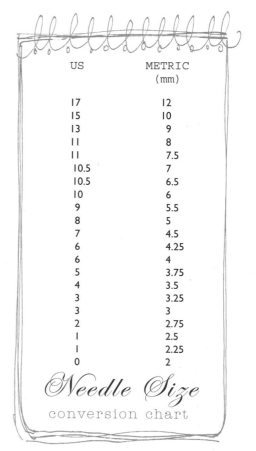

US	METRIC (mm)
17	12
15	10
13	9
11	8
11	7.5
10.5	7
10.5	6.5
10	6
9	5.5
8	5
7	4.5
6	4.25
6	4
5	3.75
4	3.5
3	3.25
3	3
2	2.75
1	2.5
1	2.25
0	2

Needle Size
conversion chart

Yarns

There are so many types of yarn to choose from—the selection can be both exciting and over-whelming! To make sense of it all, yarn is organized in a few simple ways: the fiber it's made from (such as wool, cotton, or silk), its texture (smooth, bumpy, thick-and-thin), and its thickness, or weight.

Each pattern in this book calls for a certain type of yarn, then lists the exact brand and color used. If you want to substitute a different color, go for it! And if you want to use a different yarn, that's fine too. The trick is to make sure that the yarn you use is the same basic weight as the one called for in the pattern.

The Craft Yarn Council of America has designed a system for classifying yarn weights (see the table below). Whenever you want to substitute a yarn, just make sure your yarn is in the same weight category as the one in the pattern. And before you start, *always* knit a swatch to check your gauge, using the same size needles and the same basic stitch pattern used for the body of the project (for more on checking your gauge, see page 17).

The Craft Yarn Council of America's Standard Yarn Weight System

Yarn weight symbol and name of category	1 SUPER FINE	2 FINE	3 LIGHT	4 MEDIUM	5 BULKY	6 SUPER BULKY
Types of yarn	Sock, fingering, baby	Sport, baby	DK, light worsted	Worsted, afghan, aran	Chunky, craft, rug	Bulky, roving
No. of stitches in 4 inches (in stockinette stitch)	27–32 sts	23–26 sts	21–24 sts	16–20 sts	12–15 sts	6–11 sts
Recommended needle sizes (U.S.)	1–3	3–5	5–7	7–9	9–11	11 and larger
Recommended needle sizes (metric)	2.25–3.25mm	3.25–3.75mm	3.75–4.5mm	4.5–5.5mm	5.5–8mm	8mm and larger

cotton - *lovely in summertime*

Here are just a few examples of the fabulous fibers you can choose from.

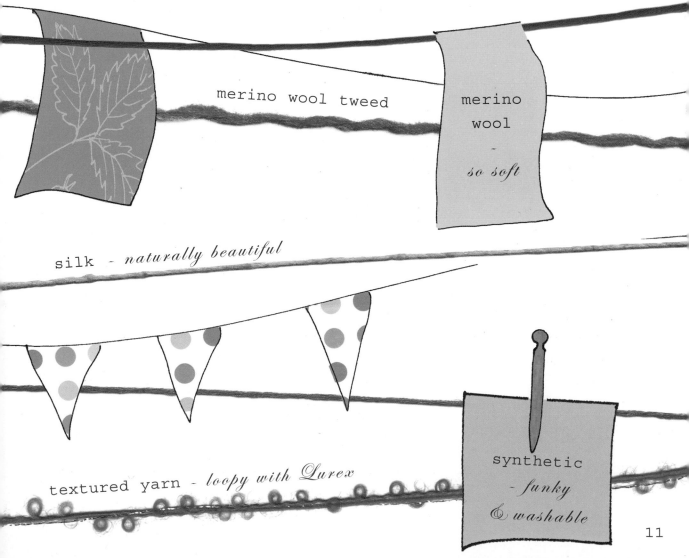

merino wool tweed

merino wool - *so soft*

silk - *naturally beautiful*

textured yarn - *loopy with Lurex*

synthetic - *funky & washable*

a.

b.

holding the yarn

c.

d.

holding the needles

Knitting Techniques

e.

f.

slip knot

g.

h.

i.

casting on

j.

k.

l.

How to get started...

There are many ways of holding needles and yarn, but it is important to hold them in the position most comfortable for you while at the same time achieving the correct gauge (see page 17). Note that the directions below are for right-handed knitters. If you are left-handed, switch the hands so your dominant hand is used to warp the yarn.

holding the yarn & needles
There are two methods of holding the yarn and needles.

the yarn:
✳ Wrap the working yarn around the little finger of your right hand (to control the tension), and pass it under the third and middle fingers and over the index finger, using the index finger to knit (*illus. a*).
✳ Pass the working yarn under the little finger of your right hand (the tension is controlled by gripping the yarn in the crook of the little finger), and pass it over the third finger, under the middle finger, and over the index finger, using the index finger to knit (*illus. b*).

the needles:
✳ Hold the needle in the right hand and the needle in the left hand as shown in *illus. c*.
✳ Hold the needle in the right hand as if holding a pen or pencil. For the first few rows the knitting will slide along the needle between the thumb and index finger. As the knitting gets longer the thumb should be held under the knit fabric. Hold the needle in the left hand as shown in *illus. d*.

making a slip knot
1 Make a loop in the yarn, and with the point of a needle pull the working yarn through the loop (*illus. e*).
2 Pull on the yarn to tighten the knot. This is the first stitch (*illus. f*).

casting on
There are several methods for casting on. This one—the cable cast on—gives a firm, neat edge.
1 Make a slip knot and place onto left-hand (LH) needle. This is the first stitch (*illus. g*).
2 Insert right-hand (RH) needle into front of slip knot. With the index finger of your right hand wrap yarn from back to front around point of needle (*illus. h*) and pull yarn toward you through slip knot to form another loop (*illus. i*). Place new loop onto LH needle. This is the second stitch (*illus. j*).
3 Insert RH needle from front to back between first and second loop on LH needle. Wrap yarn from back to front around point of RH needle and pull yarn toward you between the two stitches to form another loop (*illus. k*). Place new loop onto LH needle (*illus. l*).
4 Repeat step 3 until required number of stitches are on LH needle.

a.

b.

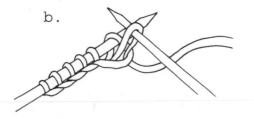

c.

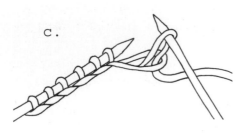

the knit stitch

think of *purl* as **knit** in reverse

d.

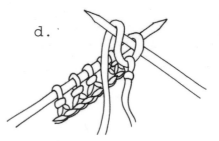

e.

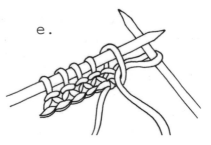

f.

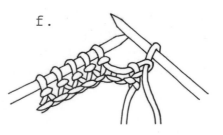

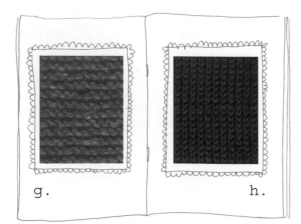

garter & stockinette stitches

the purl stitch

the knit stitch

Knit stitches are worked with the working yarn at the back of the knitting.

1 Hold needle with cast-on stitches in your left hand. Insert RH needle into front of first stitch (*illus. a*). With index finger of right hand wrap yarn from right to left around point of RH needle and pull yarn toward you through the stitch to form another loop (*illus. b*).

2 Keep new loop on RH needle while at the same time dropping original stitch off LH needle (*illus. c*).

3 Repeat steps 1 and 2 until all stitches are on RH needle. Turn RH needle around and hold in left hand so you are ready to work the next row.

the purl stitch

Purl stitches are worked with the working yarn at the front of the knitting.

1 Hold needle with stitches in left hand. Insert RH needle into first stitch from back to front and from right to left. With index finger of right hand wrap yarn from right to left around point of RH needle (*illus. d*) and pull yarn away from you through the stitch to form another loop (*illus. e*).

2 Keep new loop on RH needle while at the same time dropping original stitch off LH needle (*illus. f*).

3 Repeat steps 1 and 2 until all stitches are on RH needle. Turn RH needle around and hold in left hand so you are ready to work the next row.

Knit and purl stitches are combined to make knit fabrics. Garter stitch (knit every row) is considered the simplest knit fabric (*illus. g*). Knit stitches produce a ridge at the back of the row while purl stitches produce a ridge at the front of the row. Alternate rows of knit and purl stitches form stockinette stitch, which is smooth on one side (*illus. h*) and ridged on the other.

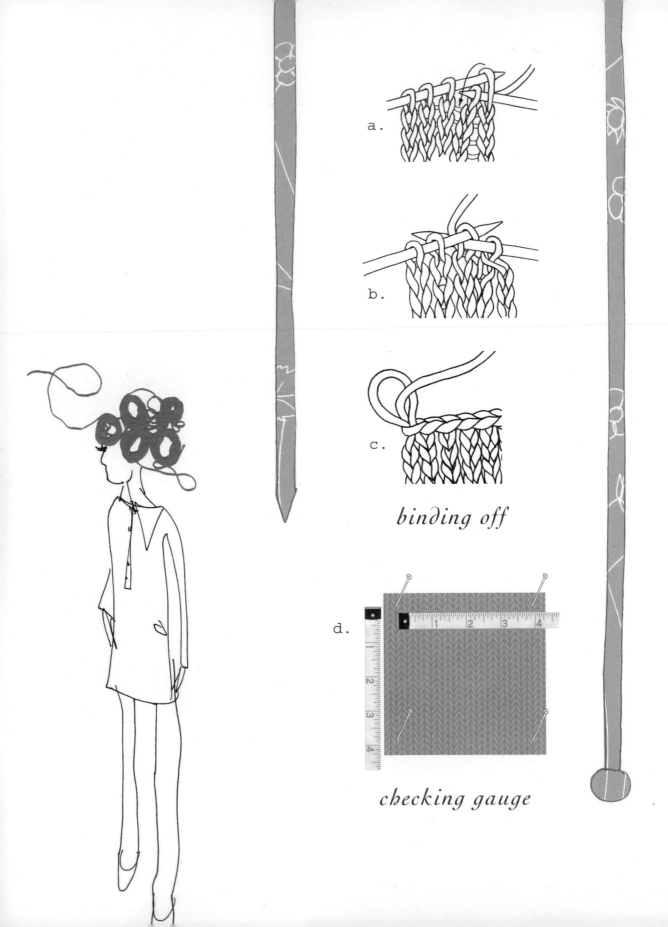

a.

b.

c.

binding off

d.

checking gauge

binding off

To finish a knit piece, you must bind off. Doing so secures your last row and takes the stitches off the needle. When you bind off, you usually work in the same stitch as the stitch pattern of the knitting. For example, if the bind-off row would have been a knit row, the stitches are bound off knitwise; if the bind-off row would have been worked in rib, the stitches are bound off knitwise and purlwise to follow the rib.

1   Knit or purl two stitches (depending on the stitch pattern) from LH needle to RH needle.

2   Using point of LH needle, pass first stitch worked over second stitch worked. One stitch has been bound off and one stitch remains on RH needle (*illus. a*).

3   Knit or purl one stitch (depending on the stitch pattern) from LH needle to RH needle (*illus. b*).

4   Using point of LH needle, pass stitch already on RH needle over stitch just worked.

5   Repeat steps 3 and 4 until there are no more stitches on LH needle and one stitch remains on RH needle.

6   Cut yarn and pull loose end through the remaining stitch on RH needle. Pull end to tighten (*illus. c*).

checking your gauge

Gauge is the number of stitches and number of rows to a 4 x 4 in./10 x 10cm square of knitting. Knitting patterns are calculated using this gauge, so checking your gauge by making a gauge swatch (*illus. d*) before you knit a garment is essential.

1   Make the gauge swatch approximately 6 x 6 in./15 x 15cm in the stitch pattern stated in the pattern. Block swatch (see page 18).

2   Measure the swatch 4 in./10cm horizontally along a row and mark with straight pins. Measure swatch 4 in./10cm vertically down the rows and mark with straight pins.

3   Count the number of stitches and rows between straight pins.

4   Check the gauge against the gauge given in the pattern. If there are too few stitches or too few rows to 4 in./10cm, use smaller needles. If there are too many stitches or too many rows to 4 in./10cm, use larger needles.

joining new yarn

Always join a new ball of yarn at the beginning of a row unless the pattern says otherwise. Do not join a new ball at an edge that will not be seamed (a free edge). At the end of the row cut the old ball of yarn to leave a tail of 6–8 in./15–20cm. Start the next row with the new ball of yarn, leaving a tail of 6–8 in./15–20cm. These tails can be knotted together.

Finishing

It is worth spending the time to finish your knitting carefully and neatly.

blocking

Knit pieces should be blocked before being sewn together.

1   Lay a piece of padding (for example, an old blanket) on a flat surface and cover with a white towel. With wrong side of knitting faceup, pin each piece to the size indicated in the pattern, making sure that rows and columns of stitches are straight. Pins should be at right angles to knitting (*illus. a*). Do not pin ribs (unless stated), and let knitting narrow toward ribbed areas.

2   Spray knitting until damp, avoiding ribs. Cover with a clean towel and pat gently to absorb excess water. Remove towel and let dry.

weaving in ends

Untie knots and weave in tails (also called ends) with a tapestry needle along side edges, bound-off edges, or on wrong side where weaving in will not show. If ends are in different colors, weave in each end along its own color. When joining yarn in middle of row or at a free edge (see page 17), weave in ends before blocking.

joining seams

Seams should be joined with the same yarn as the knit fabric or with the main yarn if more than one yarn is used. If the yarn is very thick or textured, use a thinner or smooth yarn in a matching color.

mattress stitch seam

This type of seam is suitable for any stitch pattern.

1   Place the two pieces of knit fabric to be joined next to each other, with right sides faceup and cast-on edge closest to you.

2   Between each stitch there is a "bar" made by the yarn. Thread tapestry needle with seaming yarn. Starting at cast-on edge, pick up bar between first and second stitch on right-hand piece of knitting. Pick up first bar between first and second stitch on left-hand piece of knitting (*illus. b*).

3   Return to right-hand piece of knitting and insert needle where it came out and pick up next bar. Return to left-hand piece of knitting and insert needle where it came out and pick up next bar (*illus. c*).

4   After every ¾–1¼ in./2–3cm, pull seaming yarn tightly to close seam. Repeat steps 2–4 until seam is completed.

invisible weave seam on garter stitch fabric

This gives an almost invisible finish to garter stitch fabric.

1   Place the two pieces of knit fabric to be joined next to each other, with right sides faceup and cast-on edge closest to you.

2   Thread tapestry needle with seaming yarn. Starting at cast-on edge, insert needle from bottom to top (from direction of cast-on edge toward direction of bound-off edge) through first loop on right-hand piece of knitting.

3   Insert needle from bottom to top through first loop on left-hand piece of knitting.

4   Return to right-hand piece and insert needle from bottom to top through next loop.

5   Return to left-hand piece and insert needle from bottom to top through next loop (*illus. d*).

6   After every ¾–1¼ in./2–3cm, pull seaming yarn tightly to close seam. Repeat steps 4–6 until seam is complete.

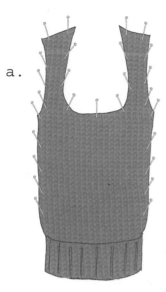

a.

blocking

b.

mattress stitch seam

c.

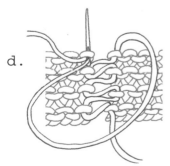

d.

invisible weave seam on garter stitch fabric

Abbreviations

alt	alternate
beg	begin(ning)
cont	continue
dec	decrease(ing)
foll	following
inc	increase(ing)
k	knit
k2tog	knit 2 sts tog
k2tog tbl	knit 2 sts tog through back loops
LH	left hand
m1	make 1 st by picking up bar before next st and knitting Into back of it
p	purl
p2tog	purl 2 sts tog
p2tog tbl	purl 2 sts tog through back loops
patt	pattern
pm	place marker
psso	pass slipped st over
rem	remain(ing)
rep	repeat(s)
RH	right hand
RS	right side (public side)
skp	slip 1 st, knit 1 st, pass slipped st over knit st
sl1k	slip 1 st knitwise
sl1p	slip 1 st purlwise
sl1wyib	slip 1 st with yarn at back of st
sl1wyif	slip 1 st with yarn at front of st
ssk	slip, slip, knit. Slip next 2 sts knitwise 1 st at a time from LH needle to RH needle. Insert LH needle from back to front through both sts and knit both sts tog
ssp	slip, slip, purl. Slip next 2 sts knitwise 1 st at a time from LH needle to RH needle. Return sts to LH needle without twisting, then p2tog tbl
st(s)	stitch(es)
St st	stockinette stitch (knit 1 row, purl 1 row)
tbl	through back loop(s)
tog	together
WS	wrong side
wyib	with yarn in back
wyif	with yarn in front
yo	yarn over needle
yo2	yarn over needle twice
*	repeat instructions after asterisk or between astrisks for as many times as patt indicates
[]	repeat instructions between brackets for as many times as patt indicates

01 fingerless gloves

These gloves bring together everything that is lovely – lace, ribbon, pearl buttons, and the beautifully simple stockinette stitch. And then there is something about fingerless gloves that is SO desirable! Each glove is knit on two needles with the thumb worked as part of the glove.

To make the gloves

Using size 3 (3mm) needles, cast on 57 sts.
Row 1 (RS): *K1, p1; rep from * to last st, k1.
Row 2: P1, *k1, p1; rep from * to end. Rows 1 and 2 form K1 P1 rib patt.

To make the wrist
Row 1 (dec row) [RS]: K27, k2tog, k28. 56 sts.
Row 2: Purl.
Row 3: Knit.
Row 4: Purl. Rows 3 and 4 form St st.
Work 30 more rows in St st, pm at each end of the 11th row of these 30 rows.

To increase for the thumb
Row 1: K27, pm, m1, k2, m1, pm, k27. 58 sts.
Row 2: Purl, slip markers from LH needle to RH needle.
Row 3: K27, slip marker, m1, k4, m1, slip marker, k27. 60 sts.
Row 4: As row 2.
Row 5: K27, slip marker, m1, k6, m1, slip marker, k27. 62 sts.
Row 6: As row 2.
Cont in St st, inc on every knit row until 22 sts between markers, end with purl row. 76 sts.
Next row (RS): Knit, removing markers.
Next row: Purl.

To complete the thumb
Row 1 (RS): K48, turn. Leave rem 28 sts on needle.
Row 2: P20 for thumb, turn. Leave 2nd set of rem 28 sts on needle. Work on 20 sts only for thumb. Beg with knit row, work 6 rows St st, dec 1 st at end of last row by p2tog. 19 sts.
Next row (RS): *K1, p1; rep from * to last st, k1.
Next row: P1, *k1, p1; rep from * to end.
Bind off in K1 P1 rib patt.

To complete the hand
With RS facing, rejoin yarn to base of thumb and knit across 28 sts on LH needle. 56 sts on RH needle. Beg with purl row, work 9 rows St st on all 56 sts, end with purl row and dec 1 st at end of last row by p2tog. 55 sts.
Next row (RS): *K1, p1; rep from * to last st, k1.
Next row: P1, *k1, p1; rep from * to end.
Bind off in K1 P1 rib patt.

To finish

Block gloves (see page 18). Sew thumb seam and glove side seam between markers and bound-off edge. Remove markers. Sew lace and ribbon at top and bottom of glove. Sew on buttons. Using size 2 (2.75mm) needles, make 2 short lengths of 1-st knit cord as follows: cast on 1 st and k onto RH needle. Insert LH needle from front to back into st and slip st onto LH needle. K this st onto RH needle. Rep for desired length. Fasten off. Sew into place for button loop.

02 scarf

There is something fabulous about this scarf—maybe the way it holds its shape around the neck, or the garter stitch pattern, or the cute way you can tuck one side through a slit in the other. . . . Knit in two gorgeous colors but with only one stitch, it is perfectly easy to make. Wrap up warm, baby.

To make the scarf

Using size 8 (5mm) needles and yarn A, cast on 25 sts.

Row 1: Knit.

Row 1 repeated forms garter st. Cont in garter st until scarf measures 7 in./18cm from cast-on edge, ending with RS row.

Next row (WS): K5, bind off 15 sts, k4. 10 sts. Cut yarn A. Join yarn B.

Next row (RS): K5, cast on 15 sts, k5. 25 sts.

Cont in garter st for another 23¾ in./60cm, ending with WS row.

Scarf measures 30¾ in./78cm from cast-on edge. Cut yarn B. Rejoin yarn A.

Cont in garter st for another 7 in./18cm, ending with a RS row.

Scarf measures 37¾ in./96cm from cast-on edge. Bind off (on WS).

To finish

Weave in loose ends and block (see page 18).

(see page 18)

what you need:

tools:
pair size 8 (5mm) knitting needles
tapestry needle

materials:
yarn A: 1 x 1¾ oz./50g ball worsted weight yarn (109 yd./100m per ball)
* we used Lana Grossa Royal Tweed, shade 25 in Orange (100% merino wool)
yarn B: 2 x 1¾ oz./50g balls worsted weight yarn (109 yd./100m per ball)
* we used Lana Grossa Royal Tweed, shade 26 in Pink (100% merino wool)

gauge & measurements:
18 sts & 36 rows = 4 in./10cm
length: 37¾ in./96cm
width: 5½ in./14cm
width of split: 3⅓ in./8.5cm

the slit is made by binding off 15 stitches

03 striped top

This is GREAT thrown over jeans, with a bracelet on your arm and a spring in your step. The sleeves are made over only 16 rows with decreases in nearly every row. Can sleeves be this cute and easy? Yes they can!

To make the back

Using size 7 (4.5mm) needles and yarn A, cast on 73 (77, 83) sts.
Work in striped rib as foll:
Row 1 (RS): *K1, p1; rep from * to last st, k1.
Row 2 (WS): P1, *k1, p1; rep from * to end.
These 2 rows form K1 P1 rib patt.
Drop yarn A. Join yarn B.
Rows 3–4: Rep rows 1 and 2.
Cut yarn B. Pick up yarn A.
Rows 5–6: Rep rows 1 and 2.
Cut yarn A. Join yarn C.
Cont in K1 P1 rib patt until work measures 3 in./ 7.5cm from cast-on edge, ending with WS row.
Change to size 9 (5.5mm) needles and St st while at same time working stripe patt, which is worked throughout as foll:

2 rows yarn A.
2 rows yarn B.
2 rows yarn A.
10 rows yarn C.

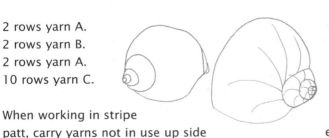

When working in stripe patt, carry yarns not in use up side of work.

what you need:

tools:
pair each sizes 7 & 9 (4.5mm & 5.5mm) knitting needles
stitch holders
tapestry needle

materials:
yarn A: 3 (3, 4) 1¾ oz./50g balls thick worsted/thin bulky weight yarn (87 yd./ 80m per ball)
* we used Lana Grossa Bingo, shade 96 in Bright Pink (100% merino wool)
yarn B: 1 (1, 2) 1¾ oz./50g balls thick worsted/thin bulky weight yarn (87 yd./ 80m per ball)
* we used Lana Grossa Bingo, shade 92 in Light Blue (100% merino wool)
yarn C: 4 (4, 5) 1¾ oz./50g balls (thick worsted/thin bulky weight yarn (87 yd./ 80m per ball)
* we used Lana Grossa Bingo, shade 33 in Chocolate Brown (100% merino wool)

gauge & measurements:
St st: 18 sts & 23 rows = 4 in./10cm
to fit bust: (small) 33½ in./85cm; (medium) 35 in./89cm; (large) 37¾ in./96cm
length to back neck (without neckband): (small) 19¾ in./50.5cm; (medium) 20 in./ 51cm; (large) 20¼ in./51.5cm

Twist yarn to be used for next knit row around yarns not in use.
Row 1 (RS): Knit.
Row 2 (WS): Purl. These 2 rows form St st.
Cont in St st and stripe patt, dec 1 st at each end of next row and every foll alt row to 63 (67, 73) sts. Dec on knit (RS) rows as foll: K4, ssk, knit to last 6 sts, k2tog, k4. Work 5 rows without shaping, beg and end with purl (WS) row.
Cont in St st and stripe patt, inc 1 st at each end of next row and every foll 4th row to 77 (81, 87) sts.

Inc on knit (RS) rows as foll: K5, m1, knit to last 5 sts, m1, k5. Cont in St st and stripe patt until back measures 10¾ (10¾, 10¾) in./27.5 (27.5, 27.5) cm, end with purl (WS) row. **

To shape the armholes

Cont in St st. Maintain stripe patt throughout.

Rows 1 and 2: Bind off 5 sts at beg of these 2 rows. 67 (71, 77) sts.

Row 3: K1, k2tog, knit to last 3 sts, ssk, k1. 65 (69, 75) sts.

Row 4: P1, ssp, purl to last 3 sts, p2tog, p1. 63 (67, 73) sts.

Row 5: K1, k2tog, knit to last 3 sts, ssk, k1. 61 (65, 71) sts.

Row 6: Purl.

Dec 1 st at each end of next row then foll 0 (1, 3) alt rows. 59 (61, 63) sts.

Cont in St st and stripe patt without shaping until armhole measures 8 (8¼, 8½) in./20.5 (21, 21.5) cm. Back should measure 18¾ (19, 19¼) in./48 (48.5, 49) cm to cast-on edge.

To shape the shoulder

Bind off 5 (5, 5) sts at beg of next 6 rows.
Bind off rem 29 (31, 33) sts.

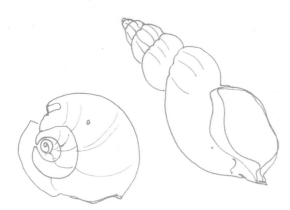

To make the front

Work as for back to **.

To shape the armholes and neck

Cont in St st. Maintain stripe patt throughout.

Row 1 (RS): Bind off 5 sts (armhole edge), k18 (19, 21) sts. 19 (20, 22) sts on RH needle. Leave rem 53 (56, 60) sts on stitch holder and work on 19 (20, 22) sts only.

Row 2: Purl.

Row 3: K1, k2tog, knit to last 3 sts, ssk, k1. 17 (18, 20) sts.

Row 4: P1, ssp, purl to last 3 sts, p2tog, p1. 15 (16, 18) sts.

Row 5: K1, k2tog, knit to last 3 sts, ssk, k1. 13 (14, 16) sts.

Row 6: Purl.

Row 7: K1, k2tog, knit to last 3 sts, ssk, k1. 11 (12, 14) sts.

Size small only:

Row 8: Purl.

Row 9: Knit to last 3 sts, ssk, k1. 10 sts.

Row 10: Purl.

Size medium only:

Row 8: Purl.

Row 9: K1, k2tog, knit to last 3 sts, ssk, k1. 10 sts.

Row 10: Purl.

Size large only:

Row 8: Purl.

Row 9: K1, k2tog, knit to last 3 sts, ssk, k1. 12 sts.

Row 10: Purl.

Row 11: K1, k2tog, knit to end. 11 sts.

Row 12: Purl.

Rows 13–14: Rep rows 11 and 12. 10 sts.

All sizes:

Cont in St st and stripe patt, inc 1 st at neck edge on 7th (7th, 3rd) row and every foll 6th row to 15 (15, 15) sts. Inc on knit (RS) rows as foll: Knit to last 5 sts, m1, k5. Cont in St st and stripe patt until armhole measures 8 (8¼, 8½) in./20.5 (21, 21.5) cm, ending with purl (WS) row. Left side of front should measure 18¾ (19, 19¼) in./48 (48.5, 49) cm to cast-on edge.

To shape the left shoulder

Row 1 (RS): Bind off 5 sts, knit to end. 10 sts.

Row 2: Purl.

Rows 3–4: Rep rows 1 and 2 once. 5 sts.
Bind off rem 5 sts.

Return to 53 (56, 60) sts left on holder.
Leave center 29 (31, 33) sts on another holder for front neck. Cont in St st and stripe patt. Knit across the rem 24 (25, 27) sts.

Row 1 (WS): Bind off 5 (5, 5) sts at beg of row (armhole edge), purl to end. 19 (20, 22) sts.

Row 2: K1, k2tog, knit to last 3 sts, ssk, k1.
17 (18, 20) sts.

Row 3: P1, ssp, purl to last 3 sts, p2tog, p1.
15 (16, 18) sts.

Row 4: K1, k2tog, knit to last 3 sts, ssk, k1.
13 (14, 16) sts.

Row 5: Purl.

Row 6: K1, k2tog, knit to last 3 sts, ssk, k1.
11 (12, 14) sts.

Size small only:

Row 7: Purl.

Row 8: K1, k2tog, knit to end. 10 sts.

Row 9: Purl.

Size medium only:

Row 7: Purl.

Row 8: K1, k2tog, knit to last 3 sts, ssk, k1.
10 sts.

Row 9: Purl.

Size large only:

Row 7: Purl.

Row 8: K1, k2tog, knit to last 3 sts, ssk, k1.
12 sts.

Row 9: Purl.

Row 10: Knit to last 3 sts, ssk, k1. 11 sts.

Row 11: Purl.

Rows 12–13: Rep rows 10 and 11. 10 sts.

All sizes:

Cont in St st and stripe patt, inc 1 st at neck edge on 7th (7th, 3rd) row and every foll 6th row to 15 (15, 15) sts.

Inc on knit (RS) rows as foll: K5, m1, knit to end. Cont in St st and stripe patt until armhole measures 8 (8¼, 8½) in./20.5 (21, 21.5) cm, end with knit (RS) row. Right side of front should measure 18¾ (19, 19¼) in./48 (48.5, 49) cm to cast-on edge.

To shape the right shoulder

Row 1 (WS): Bind off 5 sts, purl to end. 10 sts.

Row 2: Knit.

Rows 3–4: Rep rows 1 and 2 once. 5 sts.
Bind off rem 5 sts.

To make the sleeves

Using size 9 (5.5mm) needles and yarn A, cast on 133 (135, 137) sts.

Work in striped rib as foll:

Row 1 (RS): *K1, p1; rep from * to last st, k1. Drop yarn A. Join yarn B.

Row 2 (WS): P1, *k1, p1; rep from * to end. Cut yarn B. Pick up yarn A.

Row 3: *K1, p1; rep from * to last st, k1. Cut yarn A. Join yarn C.

Row 4: Purl.

To shape the sleeve top

Cont in yarn C only.

Row 1 (RS): Bind off 5 sts, K7, ssk, k10, k2tog, k6, ssk, k14, k2tog, k6, ssk, k15 (17, 19), k2tog, k6, ssk, k14, k2tog, k6, ssk, k10, k2tog, k13. 118 (120, 122) sts.

Row 2: Bind off 5 sts, purl to end. 113 (115, 117) sts.

Row 3: K1, k2tog, k5, ssk, k8, k2tog, k6, ssk, k12, k2tog, k6, ssk, k13 (15, 17), k2tog, k6, ssk, k12, k2tog, k6, ssk, k8, k2tog, k5, ssk, k1. 101 (103, 105) sts.

Row 4: P1, ssp, purl to last 3 sts, p2tog, p1. 99 (101, 103) sts.

Row 5: K1, k2tog, k3, ssk, k6, k2tog, k6, ssk, k10, k2tog, k6, ssk, k11 (13, 15), k2tog, k6, ssk, k10, k2tog, k6, ssk, k6, k2tog, k3, ssk, k1. 87 (89, 91) sts.

Row 6: P1, ssp, purl to last 3 sts, p2tog, p1. 85 (87, 89) sts.

Row 7: K1, k2tog, k1, ssk, k4, k2tog, k6, ssk, k8, k2tog, k6, ssk, k9 (11, 13), k2tog, k6, ssk, k8, k2tog, k6, ssk, k4, k2tog, k1, ssk, k1. 73 (75, 77) sts.

Row 8: Purl.

Row 9: Bind off 6 sts, k8, ssk, k6, k2tog, k6, ssk, k7 (9, 11), k2tog, k6, ssk, k6, k2tog, k15. 61 (63, 65) sts.

Row 10: Bind off 6 sts, purl to end. 55 (57, 59) sts.

Row 11: Bind off 6 sts, k2, ssk, k4, k2tog, k6, ssk, k5 (7, 9), k2tog, k6, ssk, k4, k2tog, k9. 43 (45, 47) sts.

Row 12: Bind off 6 sts, purl to end. 37 (39, 41) sts.

Row 13: Bind off 6 sts, k8, ssk, k3 (5, 7), k2tog, k15. 29 (31, 33) sts.

Row 14: Bind off 6 sts, purl to end. 23 (25, 27) sts.

Row 15: Bind off 6 sts, k2, ssk, k1 (3, 5), k2tog, k9. 15 (17, 19) sts.

Row 16: Bind off 6 sts, purl to end. 9 (11, 13) sts. Bind off rem sts.

To finish

Block each piece (including ribs of sleeves but not front and back ribs). Join right shoulder seam.

Make the neckband:

With RS facing, size 7 (4.5mm) needles, and yarn C, starting at left shoulder pick up and knit (see below) 43 (44, 46) sts along left front neck, knit across 29 (31, 33) sts left on holder at front neck, pick up and knit 44 (45, 47) sts along right front neck, pick up and knit 29 (31, 33) sts left across back neck. 145 (151, 159) sts. Start and end with 2nd (WS) row and working back and forth, work 7 rows in K1 P1 rib patt as given for back and foll stripe sequence: 4 rows yarn C, 1 row yarn A, 1 row yarn B, 1 row yarn A. Bind off in rib using yarn A.

Join left shoulder seam and neckband seam. Insert sleeves and join side and sleeve seams.

To pick up stitches

01: Hold knit fabric in LH with RS facing and needle in RH as if to knit. Sts are picked up from R to L.

02: Divide edge to be knit into sections. For example, if you have to pick up 28 sts, divide edge into quarters and pick up 7 sts in each quarter. (If picking up sts from side edge of St st, pick up 3 st for every 4 rows.)

03: When picking up from side edge, insert needle into gap between first and 2nd st at side edge. Wind yarn around needle as if to knit st, then bring yarn through knitting as if you have knit a st from LH needle. 1 st knit.

Cont until required number of sts are on RH needle.

04: When picking up at cast-on or bound-off edge, work as before but insert needle under loops of that edge. Make sure needle is inserted into gap between strands of yarn that are making sts of knit fabric and not through these strands.

- Go on, add a pom-pom!

04 cap

$\mathcal{T}$his cap is easy to knit on big needles, using a K2 P2 rib pattern and a super bulky yarn. The brim is worked in garter stitch to make a firm fabric and shade your lovely eyes. You could make this for someone special . . . but it's hard to give away the perfect winter cap. Oh well – that's love.

$\mathcal{T}$o make the cap

Using size 17 (12mm) needles, cast on 45 sts.
Row 1 (RS): *K2, p2; rep from * to last st, k1.
Row 2: P1, *k2, p2; rep from * to end. Rows 1 and 2 form K2 P2 rib patt. Work 10 more rows in K2 P2 rib patt.

To shape the top
Row 1 (RS): *K2, p2tog; rep from * to last st, k1. 34 sts.
Row 2: P1, *k1, p2tog; rep from * to end. 23 sts.
Row 3: K1, *k2tog; rep from * to end. 12 sts.
Cut yarn and thread through tapestry needle. Use tapestry needle to thread yarn through 12 sts rem on needle. Remove needle and pull to gather sts. Secure yarn. With RS facing, pm on cast-on row 15 sts from LH edge and another 14 sts from RH edge. 16 sts between markers.

To turn garter st short rows

01: K number of sts stated before turn. Slip first st on LH needle to RH needle without knitting it. Bring yarn from back to front between needles. Slip same st back from RH needle to LH needle.
02: Turn needles around. Yarn will be in correct position for next garter-st row and slipped st is now "wrapped" by yarn. When knitting wrapped slipped st on next row, k st and wrap tog.

what you need:

tools:
pair each sizes 10.5 & 17 (7mm & 12mm) knitting needles
tapestry needle
stitch markers
sewing needle & thread

materials:
2 x 3½ oz./100g balls super bulky weight yarn (33 yd./30m per ball)
* we used Rowan Biggy Print, shade 260 in Green/Blue (100% merino wool)

gauge & measurements:
K2 P2 rib patt: 9 sts & 10 rows = 4 in./10cm
garter st: 10 sts & 20 rows = 4 in./10cm
to fit average-sized head

To make the brim
Using size 10.5 (7mm) needles, cast on 23 sts.
Shape using short rows (see below left) as foll:
Row 1 (WS): Knit.
Row 2: K15, turn.
Row 3: K7, turn.
Row 4: K9, turn.
Row 5: K11, turn.
Row 6: K13, turn.
Row 7: K15, turn.
Row 8: K16, turn.
Row 9: K17, turn.
Row 10: K18, turn.
Row 11: K19, turn.
Row 12: K20, turn.
Row 13: K21, turn.
Row 14: K22, turn.
Bind off all 23 sts (on WS).

$\mathcal{T}$o finish

Join cap seam, but only join half of the sts. With RS faceup, sew bound-off edge of brim to cast-on edge of cap between markers.

05 biker shrug

Yes, this is fabulously pretty – but also just a bit rock 'n' roll. The eyelet pattern and fluffy yarn create a cute, lacy fabric and the sleeves puff out just a little in that *oh-so-gorgeous* way. Fasten with a twinkly diamanté buckle and be your very own road movie heroine!

To make the back

Using size 11 (7.5mm) needles, cast on 37 (41, 41) sts.

Row 1 (RS): *K1, p1; rep from * to last st, k1.

Row 2: P1, *k1, p1; rep from * to end. Rows 1 and 2 form K1 P1 rib patt.

Rows 3–5: Work 3 more rows in K1 P1 rib patt.

Row 6 (WS): Purl, inc 1 st in the center of row for size small only. 38 (41, 41) sts.

To shape the back

Shaping is worked in short rows (see page 35).

Row 1 (RS): K6 (7, 7), turn.

Row 2: P6 (7, 7) sts.

Row 3: K12 (14, 14), turn.

Row 4: P12 (14, 14) sts.

Row 5: Knit across all 38 (41, 41) sts.

Row 6: P6 (7, 7), turn.

Row 7: K6 (7, 7) sts.

what you need:

tools:
pair each sizes 10.5 & 11 (7mm & 7.5mm) knitting needles
stitch markers
tapestry needle

materials:
4(4, 5) x 1¾ oz./50g balls super bulky weight yarn (71 yd./65m per ball)
* we used ggh Amelie, shade 009 in Black (100% polyamide)
2 short lengths of contrast yarn
diamanté buckle, ⅝ in./1.5cm wide

gauge & measurements:
10½ sts & 17 rows = 4 in./10cm
to fit bust: (small) 31¾ in./81cm;
(medium) 34 in./86cm; (large)
35¾ in./91cm
back length (side edge to shoulder):
(small) 5½ in./14cm; (medium)
5½ in./14cm; (large) 5½ in./14cm

Row 8: P12 (14, 14), turn.

Row 9: K12 (14, 14) sts.

Row 10: Purl across all 38 (41, 41) sts.

Shaping completed. 7 rows St st worked at each side edge and 3 rows St st worked on center 14 (13, 13) sts.

To begin the eyelet pattern

Row 1 (RS): K2, *yo, k2tog, k1; rep from * to end.

Row 2: Purl.

Row 3: Knit.

Row 4: Purl.

These 4 rows form eyelet patt.

Rows 5–8: Work 4 more rows in eyelet patt.

Row 9: K2, *yo, k2tog, k1; rep from * to end.

Row 10: Purl.

Row 11: Bind off 12 (13, 13) sts, knit to end.

Row 12: Bind off 12 (13, 13) sts, purl to end.

Bind off rem 14 (15, 15) sts.

To make the left front

Using size 11 (7.5mm) needles, cast on 13 (13, 13) sts.

Rows 1–5: Work 5 rows in K1 P1 rib patt as for back.

Row 6 (WS): Purl, dec 1 st at end of row for size small only. 12 (13, 13) sts.

To shape the left front

Shaping is worked in short rows (see page 35).

Row 1 (RS): K4 (4, 4) turn.

Row 2: P4 (4, 4) sts.

Row 3: K5 (5, 5), turn.

Row 4: P5 (5, 5) sts.

Row 5: K2, yo, k2tog, k2, turn. 6 (6, 6) sts.

Row 6: P6 (6, 6) sts.

Row 7: K8 (9, 9), turn.

Row 8: P8 (9, 9) sts.

Row 9: K2, *yo, k2tog, k1; rep from * 3 (3, 3) times, k1 (0, 0), turn. 12 (11, 11) sts.

Row 10: P12 (11, 11) sts.

Row 11: Knit across all 12 (13, 13) sts.

Row 12: Purl across all 12 (13, 13) sts.

Bind off knitwise.

To make the right front

Using size 11 (7.5mm) needles, cast on 13 (13, 13) sts.

Rows 1–5: Work 5 rows in K1 P1 rib patt as for back, dec 1 st at end of last row for size small only. 12 (13, 13) sts.

To shape the right front

Shaping is worked in short rows (see page 35).

Row 1 (WS): P4 (4, 4), turn.

Row 2: K4 (4, 4) sts.

Row 3: P5 (5, 5), turn.

Row 4: K5 (5, 5) sts.

Row 5: P6 (6, 6), turn.

Row 6: K3, yo, k2tog, k1. 6 (6, 6) sts.

Row 7: P8 (9, 9), turn.

Row 8: K8 (9, 9) sts.

Row 9: P12 (11, 11), turn.

Row 10: K3, *yo, k2tog, k1; rep from * 2 (1, 1) times, yo 0 (1, 1) time, k2tog 0 (1, 1) time. 12 (11, 11) sts.

Row 11: Purl across all 12 (13, 13) sts.

Row 12: Knit across all 12 (13, 13) sts.

Row 13: Purl across all 12 (13, 13) sts.

Bind off knitwise.

To make the sleeves

Using size 10.5 (7mm) needles, cast on 25 (25, 27) sts.

Rows 1–11: Work 11 rows in K1 P1 rib patt as for back.

Row 12 (WS): Purl, inc 4 (4, 5) sts evenly across the row. 29 (29, 32) sts.

Change to size 11 (7.5mm) needles.

To begin the eyelet pattern

Row 1 (RS): K2, *yo, k2tog, k1; rep from * to end.

Row 2: Purl.

Row 3: Knit.

Row 4: Purl.

These 4 rows form eyelet patt.

Rows 5–12: Work 8 more rows in eyelet patt.

Row 13: K1, m1, work in patt to last st, m1, k1. 31 (31, 34) sts.

Cont in eyelet patt until 48 (50, 52) rows worked in all while inc 1 st at each end of 25th (27th, 27th) and 37th (41st, 41st) rows as for 13th row, bringing extra sts into patt. 35 (35, 38) sts.

To shape the sleeve top

Maintain continuity of eyelet patt throughout.

Bind off 2 sts at beg of next 2 rows. 31 (31, 34) sts.

Row 3: K1, ssk, work in patt to last 3 sts, k2tog, k1. 29 (29, 32) sts.

Row 4: Purl.

Rep 3rd and 4th rows until 7 (7, 10) sts rem, pm at each end of last row.

Work in patt for 4 rows without shaping. Bind off. Thread contrast yarn through sleeves between markers at top. For back of sleeve, pm at side edge of sleeve top between 8th and 9th rows from underarm bind-off. For front of sleeve, pm at side edge of sleeve top between 12th and 13th rows from underarm bind-off.

To make the buckle strap

Row 1 (RS): Knit.
Row 2: Purl. Rows 1 and 2 form St st.
Rows 3–6: Work 4 more rows in St st.
Row 7: K2tog, k1, ssk. 3 sts.
Cont in St st until strap measures 2 in./5cm, ending with a purl row.
Next row: Sl 1, k2tog, psso. 1 st. Fasten off.

To finish

Block each piece (see page 18), including front and back ribs but not sleeve ribs. Join shoulder seams. Make neckband (see below). Pull contrast yarn at top of each sleeve to gather. Fold sleeves in half lengthwise and place center of bound-off edge to shoulder seam. Sew into place between markers, gathering top of sleeves to fit.

To make the neckband

Using size 11 (7.5mm) needles, cast on 11 (12, 13) sts.
Rows 1–4: Work 4 rows in St st for strap.
Row 5: K11 (12, 13), with RS facing pick up and knit (see page 29) 5 (5, 5) sts along front side edge of right front, 17 (18, 18) sts across back neck, and 5 (5, 5) sts along side edge of left front. 38 (40, 41) sts.
Work 8 rows in St st beg with purl row.

Row 13 (RS): Bind off 11 (12, 13) sts, knit to end. 27 (28, 28) sts.
Rows 14–17: Work 4 rows in St st beg with purl row and ending with knit row.
Bind off all 27 (28, 28) sts or leave on needle. Fold over neckband to WS. Working from right to left on WS of shrug, sew first bound-off st or first st left on needle to first st at base of neckband. Drop st from needle when sewn.
*Sew next bound-off st or next st left on needle to next st at base of neckband. Rep from * until all sts have been sewn into place.

fold over neckband – sewing sts that are not bound off

Sew buckle onto RS of neckband at left side. Sew to close the open side edge of neckband at left side of neck. Fold cast-on and bound-off edges of neckband extension to WS and sew edges together. Sew side edge of extension to main neckband where they meet. Insert cast-on edge of strap into open side edge of extension. Sew to close the open neck edge of extension and secure strap in place.

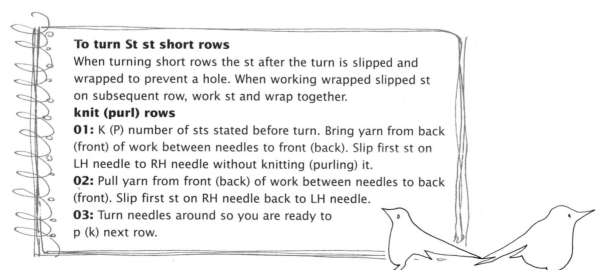

To turn St st short rows

When turning short rows the st after the turn is slipped and wrapped to prevent a hole. When working wrapped slipped st on subsequent row, work st and wrap together.

knit (purl) rows

01: K (P) number of sts stated before turn. Bring yarn from back (front) of work between needles to front (back). Slip first st on LH needle to RH needle without knitting (purling) it.
02: Pull yarn from front (back) of work between needles to back (front). Slip first st on RH needle back to LH needle.
03: Turn needles around so you are ready to p (k) next row.

06 knee warmers

Nothing to wear to the roller disco? Do not despair, these knee warmers are just the thing. Worked in garter stitch and deep rib, will these knee warmers fall down? No, they won't. Will you? Maybe . . .

To make the knee warmers

Using size 6 (4mm) needles and yarn A, cast on 53 sts.

Row 1 (RS): *K1, p1; rep from * to last st, k1.
Row 2: P1, *k1, p1; rep from * to end. Rows 1 and 2 form K1 P1 rib patt.
Cut yarn A. Join yarn B.
Work 26 rows in K1 P1 rib patt. Rib should measure 3½ in./9cm. Cut yarn B. Join yarn A.

Work 4 rows in K1 P1 rib patt. Rib should measure 4 in./10cm and finish with row 2 (WS). Cut yarn A. Join yarn B. Work 6 rows in garter st.

To shape the knee section

This is worked in short rows (see page 31).

Row 1 (RS): K51 sts, turn.
Row 2: K49 sts, turn.
Row 3: K47 sts, turn.
Row 4: K45 sts, turn.
Row 5: K43 sts, turn.
Row 6: K41 sts, turn.
Cont working in short rows, working 2 sts less in every row until:
Row 24 (WS): K5 sts, turn.
Row 25 (RS): K7 sts, turn. From now on wrapped slipped sts (see page 31) will have 2 wraps. When knitting wrapped st, knit tog with both wraps.
Row 26: K9 sts, turn.
Cont working in short rows, working 2 sts more in every row until:
Row 48 (WS): Knit across all 53 sts.
Work 6 rows in garter st across all 53 sts, end with WS row. Cut yarn B.

what you need:

tools:
pair size 6 (4mm) knitting needles
tapestry needle

materials:
yarn A: 1 x 1¾ oz./50g ball mohair worsted weight yarn (110 yd./100m per ball)
* we used Be Sweet Bouclé Mohair in Acid Green (100% baby mohair)
yarn B: 2 x 1¾ oz./50g balls mohair worsted weight yarn (110 yd./100m per ball)
* we used Be Sweet Bouclé Mohair in Bright Pink (100% baby mohair)

gauge & measurements:
21½ sts & 43 rows = 4 in./10cm
front knee length: 13½ in./34.5cm
back knee length: 9⅓ in./23.75cm
circumference: 10 in./25cm

To work the rib for the top

Join yarn A.
Row 1 (RS): Knit.
Row 2: P1, *k1, p1; rep from * to end.
Row 3: *K1, p1; rep from * to last st, k1.
Row 4: P1, *k1, p1; rep from * to end.
Rows 3 and 4 form K1 P1 rib patt. Cut yarn A. Join yarn B. Work 26 rows in K1 P1 rib patt. Rib should measure 3½ in./9cm. Cut yarn B. Join yarn A. Work 2 rows in K1 P1 rib patt. Rib should measure 4 in./10cm and finish with row 2 (WS). Bind off loosely in rib.

To finish

Block garter st areas of knee warmers (see page 18). Join back seam. Use mattress stitch seam (see page 18) for K1 P1 ribs, but only join half of the sts. Use invisible weave seam (see page 18) for remainder of sts.

07 cardigan

Here comes spring—and here is a fabulous springtime cardigan. Knit with a simple stockinette stitch design, the front trim is knit as you go. Easy! Finish with a row of vintage buttons and go greet the sunshine.

To make the back

Using size 3 (3.25mm) needles and yarn A, cast on 93 (101, 109) sts.

Row 1 (RS): *K1, p1; rep from * to last st, k1.
Row 2: P1, *k1, p1; rep from * to end. Rows 1 and 2 form K1 P1 rib patt. Work 24 more rows in K1 P1 rib patt. Rib should measure 3 in./7.5cm.
Change to size 5 (3.75mm) needles and yarn B.
Row 1 (RS): *K5 (6, 6), m1, k6 (6, 7), m1; rep from * to last 5 sts, k5. 109 (117, 125) sts.
Row 2: Purl.
Row 3: K4, *p1, k7; rep from * to last st, k1.
Row 4: P2, *p5, k3; rep from * to last 3 sts, p3.
Row 5: As row 3.
Row 6: Purl.
Row 7: Knit.
Row 8: Purl.
Row 9: K1, *k7, p1; rep from * to last 4 sts, k4.
Row 10: P3, *k3, p5; rep from * to last 2 sts, p2.
Row 11: As row 9.
Rows 12–14: As rows 6 to 8. Rows 3 to 14 form 12-row st patt. Cont in patt for another 68 rows. 82 patt rows worked in all. Back should measure 12 in./30cm from cast-on edge.

To shape the armholes

Maintaining continuity of st patt throughout, bind off 5 sts at beg of next 2 rows. 99 (107, 115) sts. Dec 1 st at each end of next 5 (7, 9) rows. 89 (93, 97) sts. Then dec 1 st at each end of next alt row and then foll 2 (2, 2) alt rows. 83 (87, 91) sts. Work dec as foll:
RS rows: K1, k2tog, work in patt to last 3 sts, ssk, k1.

what you need:

tools:
pair each sizes 3 & 5 (3.25mm & 3.75mm) knitting needles
stitch holders
tapestry needle

materials:
yarn A: 2 (2, 3) x 1¾ oz./50g balls sport weight yarn (137 yd./125m per ball)
* we used Debbie Bliss Baby Cashmerino shade 340605 in Lavender Blue (55% merino, 33% microfiber, 12% cashmere)
yarn B: 8 (9, 9) x 1¾ oz./50g balls sport weight yarn (137 yd./125m per ball)
* we used Debbie Bliss Baby Cashmerino shade 34001 in Pale Yellow (55% merino, 33% microfiber, 12% cashmere)
7 x 1 in./15mm-diameter buttons

gauge & measurements:
25 sts & 36 rows = 4 in./10cm
to fit bust: (small) 31¾ in./81cm;
(medium) 33¾ in./86cm; (large) 35¾ in./91cm
length to shoulder: (small) 19¾ in./50cm;
(medium) 20 in./51cm; (large) 20½ in./52cm

WS rows: P1, ssp, work in patt to last 2 sts, p2tog, p1.
Cont in patt without shaping until 72 (76, 80) rows in all have been worked for armholes. Armholes should measure 8 (8¼, 8⅔) in./20 (21, 22) cm. Back should measure 19¾ (20, 20½) in./50 (51, 52) cm from cast-on edge.

To shape the shoulders

Maintain continuity of st patt.
Bind off 6 (6, 6) sts at beg of next 2 rows. 71 (75, 79) sts.
Bind off 6 (6, 7) sts at beg of next 2 rows. 59 (63, 65) sts.
Bind off 6 (7, 7) sts at beg of next 2 rows. 47 (49, 51) sts.
Bind off 7 (7, 7) sts at beg of next 2 rows.
Bind off rem 33 (35, 37) sts.

To make the left front

Using size 3 (3.25mm) needles and yarn A, cast on 51 (55, 59) sts.

Work 26 rows in K1 P1 rib patt as for back.

Change to size 5 (3.75mm) needles and yarn B.

Row 1 (RS): K7 (2, 6) *m1, k4 (5, 5); rep from * to last 8 sts, rejoin yarn A and [p1, k1] 4 times. 60 (64, 68) sts.

Row 2: Using yarn A, [p1, k1] 4 times, using yarn B, purl to end.

Rows 1 and 2 set position of 8-st K1 P1 rib patt front band in yarn A and main section of front worked in st patt in yarn B. Maintain color sequence throughout. When changing colors, twist yarns together to avoid making a hole (see page 50).

Row 3: K4, *p1, k7; rep from * to last 8 (12, 8) sts, p0 (1, 0), k0 (3, 0), work 8 sts in K1 P1 rib patt.

Row 4: Work 8 sts in K1 P1 rib patt, p6 (2, 6), *k3, p5; rep from * to last 6 sts, k3, p3.

Row 5: As row 3.

Row 6: Work 8 sts in K1 P1 rib patt, purl to end.

Row 7: Knit to last 8 sts, work 8 sts in K1 P1 rib patt.

Row 8: Work 8 sts in K1 P1 rib patt, purl to end.

Row 9: K8, *p1, k7; rep from * to last 12 (8, 12) sts, p1 (0, 1), k3 (0, 3), work 8 sts in K1 P1 rib patt.

Row 10: Work 8 sts in K1 P1 rib patt, p2 (6, 2), *k3, p5; rep from * to last 2 sts, p2.

Row 11: As row 9.

Row 12-14: As rows 6 to 8.

Rows 3 to 14 form 12-row st patt. Cont in patt with rib front border for another 68 rows. 82 patt rows worked in all. Left front should measure 12 in./30cm from cast-on edge.

To shape the armholes

Maintain continuity of st patt throughout.

Row 1: Bind off 5 sts, work in patt to end. 55 (59, 63) sts.

Row 2: Work in patt.

Dec 1 st at armhole edge of the 5 (7, 9) rows. 50 (52, 54) sts. Then dec 1 st at armhole edge of next alt row and then foll 1 (2, 1) alt rows, ending with a RS row. 48 (49, 52) sts. Work dec as foll:

RS rows: K1, k2tog, work in patt to end.

WS rows: Work in patt to last 3 sts, p2tog, p1.

Work 5 (1, 1) more rows in patt without shaping.

To shape the front slope

Row 1: Work in patt to last 10 sts, k2tog, work 8 sts in K1 P1 rib patt. 47 (48, 51) sts.

Cont in patt, dec 1 st at the neck edge only on row 4 of neck shaping and every foll 3rd row of neck shaping until 15 (15, 17) sts **in all** have been decreased at neck edge. 33 (34, 35) sts. Work dec as foll:

RS rows: Work in patt to last 10 sts, k2tog, work 8 sts in K1 P1 rib patt.

WS rows: Work 8 sts in K1 P1 rib patt, p2tog, work in patt to end.

Cont in patt without shaping until 72 (76, 80) rows **in all** have been worked for armhole. Armhole should measure 8 (8¼, 8⅔) in./20 (21, 22) cm. Left front should measure 19¾ (20, 20½) in./50 (51, 52) cm from cast-on edge.

To shape the shoulders

Maintain continuity of st patt.

Bind off 6 (6, 6) sts at beg of next row. 27 (28, 29) sts. Work 1 row in patt.

Bind off 6 (6, 7) sts at beg of next row. 21 (22, 22) sts. Work 1 row in patt.

Bind off 6 (7, 7) sts at beg of next row. 15 (15, 15) sts. Work 1 row in patt.

Bind off 7 (7, 7) sts at beg of next row, leaving the 8 rib sts intact. 8 (8, 8) sts.

Using yarn A, cont in K1 P1 rib patt on rem 8 sts until rib is long enough to reach center of back neck. Leave these sts on holder.

To make the right front

Using size 3 (3.25mm) needles and yarn A, cast on 51 (55, 59) sts.

Work 4 rows in K1 P1 rib patt as for back.

Row 5 (buttonhole row): K1, p1, ssk, yo2, work in K1 P1 rib patt to end.

Work 19 more rows in K1 P1 rib patt.

Row 25: As row 5.

Work 1 more row in K1 P1 rib patt.

Change to size 5 (3.75mm) needles.

Row 1 (RS): [K1, p1] 4 times, join yarn B, *k4 (5, 5), m1; rep from * to last 3 (2, 6) sts, k7 (2, 6). 60 (64, 68) sts.

Row 2: Using yarn B, purl to last 8 sts, using yarn A, [P1, k1] 4 times.

Rows 1 and 2 set position of 8-st K1 P1 rib patt front band in yarn A and main section of front worked in st patt in yarn B. Maintain color sequence throughout. When changing colors, twist yarns together to avoid making a hole (see page 50).

Row 3: Work 8 sts in K1 P1 rib patt, k3 (0, 3), p1 (0, 1), *k7, p1; rep from * to last 8 sts, k8.

Row 4: P2, *p5, k3; rep from * to last 10 (14, 10) sts, p2 (6, 2), work 8 sts in K1 P1 rib patt.

Row 5: As row 3.

Row 6: Purl to last 8 sts, work 8 sts in K1 P1 rib patt.

Row 7: Work 8 sts in K1 P1 rib patt, knit to end.

Row 8: Purl to last 8 sts, work 8 sts in K1 P1 rib patt.

Row 9: Work 8 sts in K1 P1 rib patt, k0 (3, 0), p0 (1, 0), *k7, p1; rep from * to last 4 sts, k4.

Row 10: P3, k3, *p5, k3; rep from * to last 14 (10, 14) sts, p6 (2, 6), work 8 sts in K1 P1 rib patt.

Row 11: As row 9.

Row 12-14: As rows 6 to 8.

Rows 3 to 14 form 12-row st patt. Cont in patt with rib front border for another 68 rows **while at the same time** working a buttonhole on the 20th row from previous buttonhole.

Work buttonhole row as foll:

Buttonhole row (RS): K1, p1, yo2, work in patt to end. 82 patt rows worked in all.

Right front should measure 12 in./30cm from cast-on edge and 6 buttonholes in all made.

To shape the armholes

Maintain continuity of st patt throughout.

Row 1: Work in patt.

Row 2: Bind off 5 sts, work in patt to end. 55 (59, 63) sts.

Dec 1 st at armhole edge of next 5 (7, 9) rows. 50 (52, 54) sts. Then dec 1 st at armhole edge of next alt row and then foll 1 (2, 1) alt rows, end with RS row. 48 (49, 52) sts.

Work dec as foll:

RS rows: Work in patt to last 3 sts, ssk, k1.

WS rows: P1, ssp, work in patt to end.

Work 5 (1, 1) more rows in patt without shaping.

To shape the front slope

Row 1: K1, p1, yo2, work 4 sts in K1 P1 rib patt, ssk, work in patt to end.

7th and final buttonhole made and first front slope dec made.

Cont in patt, dec 1 st at the neck edge only on row 4 of neck shaping and every foll 3rd row of neck shaping until 15 (15, 17) sts have been decreased at neck edge. 33 (34, 35) sts.

Work dec as foll:

RS rows: Work 8 sts in K1 P1 rib patt, ssk, work in patt to end.

WS rows: Work in patt to last 10 sts, ssp, work 8 sts in K1 P1 rib patt.

Cont in patt without shaping until 72 (76, 80) rows in all have been worked for armhole. Armhole should measure 8 (8¼, 8⅔) in./ 20 (21, 22) cm. Right front should measure 19¾ (20, 20½) in./50 (51, 52) cm from cast-on edge.

To shape the shoulders

Maintain continuity of st patt.

Work 1 row in patt.

Bind off 6 (6, 6) sts at beg
of next row.
27 (28, 29) sts.

Work 1 row in patt.

Bind off 6 (6, 7) sts
at beg of next row.
21 (22, 22) sts.

Work 1 row in patt.

Bind off 6 (7, 7) sts at beg of
next row. 15 (15, 15) sts.

Work 1 row in patt.

Bind off 7 (7, 7) sts at beg of next row, leaving the
8 rib sts intact. 8 (8, 8) sts. Using yarn A, cont in
K1 P1 rib patt on rem 8 sts until rib is long enough
to reach center of back neck. Leave these sts on
holder.

To make the sleeves

Using size 3 (3.25mm) needles and yarn A, cast on
47 (49, 51) sts.

Work 26 rows in K1 P1 rib patt as for back.

Cut yarn A.

Change to size 5 (3.75mm) needles and yarn B.

Row 1: K0 (0, 1), *k7, m1; rep from * to last
5 (7, 8) sts, k5 (7, 8). 53 (55, 57) sts.

Row 2: Purl.

Row 3: K2 (3, 4), p1, *k7, p1; rep from * to last
2 (3, 4) sts, k2 (3, 4).

Row 4: P1 (2, 3), *k3, p5; rep from * to last
1 (2, 3) sts, p1 (2, 3).

Row 5: As row 3.

Row 6: Purl.

Row 7: Knit.

Row 8: Purl.

Row 9: K6 (7, 8), *p1, k1; rep from * to last 7 (8,
9) sts, p1, k6 (7, 8).

Row 10: P5 (6, 7), k3, *p5, k3; rep from * to last
5 (6, 7) sts, p5 (6, 7).

Row 11: As row 9.

Rows 12–14: As rows 6 to 8.

Rows 3 to 14 form 12-row st patt. Cont in patt for
another 114 rows, **while at the same time** inc
1 st at each end of first of these rows and every foll
8th row to 77 (79, 81) sts, working rem of rows
without shaping.

Work inc as foll:

RS rows: K1, m1, work in patt to last st, m1, k1.
128 patt rows worked in all. Sleeve should measure
17 in./43cm from cast-on edge.

To shape the sleeve top

Maintain continuity of patt throughout.

Bind off 5 sts at beg of next 2 rows. 67 (69, 71) sts.

Row 3: K1, ssk, work in patt to last 3 sts, k2tog,
k1. 65 (67, 69) sts.

Row 4: Purl.

Rep rows 3 and 4 until 15 sts rem. Bind off.

To finish

Block each piece (see page 18). Join shoulder
seams. Pm at center back neck. Make sure rib
extensions for back neckband are of equal length,
meeting at center back neck when slightly stretched
and ending with WS row. Bind off each piece. Join
rib extension seam from free edge to neck edge.
Sew back neckband into position.

Fold sleeves in half lengthwise and place center
of bound-off edge to shoulder seam. Sew sleeves
into position. Join side seams, using 1 st as the
seam allowance. Join sleeve seams, using half a
st as the seam allowance.

Sew on buttons to correspond with buttonholes.

08 dress

This dress has everything a *perfect* party dress needs—a simple shape, a pretty neckline, fun knit pom-poms and a peephole stitch pattern that is just a little risqué. Just like the perfect party. Also wonderful thrown over a bikini on the beach.

To make the back

Using size 3 (3.25mm) needles and yarn A, cast on 104 (110, 116) sts, using method for knit hem (pages 48–9) if liked.

Row 1 (RS): Knit.

Row 2: Purl.

These 2 rows form St st.

Work 4 more rows in St st. Drop yarn A.

Change to yarn B and work 2 rows in St st.

Next row (RS) [picot hem row]: K1, *yo, k2tog; rep from * to last st, k1.

Change to size 5 (3.75mm) needles.

Next row: Purl.

Cut yarn B. Rejoin yarn A. Work 6 rows in St st.

Next row (RS): Make hem (see pages 48–9).

Next row: Purl.

Begin eyelet pattern

Row 1 (RS): K3 (6, 5), [yo, ssk, k6] 12 (12, 13) times, yo, ssk, k3 (6, 5).

Rows 2, 4, 6, 8, 10, 12, 14, and 16: Purl.

Row 3: K1 (4, 3), [k2tog, yo, k1, yo, ssk, k3] 12 (12, 13) times, k2tog, yo, k1, yo, ssk, k2 (5, 4).

Row 5 (RS): K3 (6, 5), [yo, ssk, k6] 12 (12, 13) times, yo, ssk, k3 (6, 5).

Row 7: Knit.

Row 9: K7 (10, 9), [yo, ssk, k6] 12 (12, 13) times, k1 (4, 3).

Row 11: K5 (8, 7), [k2tog, yo, k1, yo, ssk, k3] 12 (12, 13) times, k3 (6, 5).

Row 13: K7 (10, 9), [yo, ssk, k6] 12 (12, 13) times, k1 (4, 3).

Row 15: Knit.

Rows 1 to 16 form patt. Cont in patt until 202 (206,

what you need:

tools:
pair each sizes 3 & 5 (3.5mm & 3.75mm) knitting needles
2 x size 2 (2.75mm) double-pointed knitting needles
stitch holders
tapestry needle

materials:
yarn A: 9 (9, 10) x 1¾ oz./50g balls sport weight yarn (120 yd./110m per ball)
* we used ggh Mystik, shade 097 in Dark Blue (54% cotton, 46% viscose)
yarn B: 1 (1, 1) x 1¾ oz./50g ball sport weight yarn (120 yd./110m per ball)
* we used ggh Mystik, shade 074 in Light Blue (54% cotton, 46% viscose)

gauge & measurements:
23 sts & 33 rows = 4 in./10cm (after blocking)
to fit bust: (small) 35 in./89cm; (medium) 37 in./94cm; (large) 39 in./99cm
length to shoulder: (small) 32 in./82cm; (medium) 33 in./84cm; (large) 34 in./87cm

212) eyelet patt rows have been worked in all. Back should measure 25 (25½, 26) in./64 (65, 67) cm from picot hem row, ending with a WS row. **

To shape the armhole

Maintain continuity of patt throughout. Bind off 5 sts at beg of next 2 rows. 94 (100, 106) sts.

Dec 1 st at each end of next 5 (7, 9) rows. 84 (86, 88) sts. Dec 1 st at each end of the next 5 alt rows. 74 (76, 78) sts.

Work dec as foll:

RS rows: K1, k2tog, work in patt to last 3 sts, ssk, k1.

WS rows: P1, ssp, work in patt to last 2 sts, p2tog, p1.

Cont without shaping until 60 (62, 66) armhole rows have been worked in all. Armholes should measure 7 (7½, 8) in./18 (19, 20) cm, ending with WS row.

Back should measure 32 (33, 34) in./82 (84, 87) cm from picot hem row.

To shape the shoulder

Bind off 6 sts at beg of next 2 rows. 62 (64, 66) sts.

Bind off 7 sts at beg of next 4 rows.

Bind off rem 34 (36, 38) sts.

To make the front

Work as for back to ** but beg eyelet patt with row 9 instead of row 1.

To shape armholes and divide for the fronts

Maintain continuity of patt throughout.

Row 1 (RS): Bind off 5 sts, work in patt for 46 (49, 52) sts. 47 (50, 53) sts on RH needle. Turn and work on these 47 (50, 53) sts only for L side of neck. Leave rem 52 (55, 58) sts on stitch holder for R side of neck.

Row 2 (WS): Work in patt.

Work 41 (43, 47) more rows in eyelet pattern **while at the same time** dec 1 st at armhole edge on the next 5 (7, 9) rows and then dec 1 st at armhole edge of foll 5 alt rows and **also at the same time** dec 1 st at neck edge on the next row and foll 7 (8, 9) 5th rows. 29 (29, 29) sts. Armhole should measure 5 (5⅓, 5¾) in./13 (13.5, 14.5) cm, ending with RS row.

Work dec as foll:

RS rows: K1, k2tog at beg of row; ssk, k1 at end of row.

WS rows: P1, ssp at beg of row; p2tog, p1 at end of row.

To shape the neck

Row 1 (WS): Bind off 3 sts, purl to end. 26 sts. Work 16 more rows in eyelet patt, dec 1 st at neck edge on the first 6 rows. 20 sts.

To shape the shoulder

Row 1 (RS): Bind off 6 sts, work in patt to end. 14 sts.

Rows 2 and 4: Purl.

Row 3: Bind off 7 sts, work in patt to end. 7 sts. Bind off rem 7 sts.

To make the right side of the neck

Row 1 (RS): With RS facing, using size 5 (3.75mm) needles, rejoin yarn A and work in patt across 52 (55, 58) sts left on stitch holder.

Row 2 (WS): Bind off 5 sts, purl to end. 47 (50, 53) sts.

Work 40 (42, 46) more rows in eyelet patt, **at same time** as working shapings to match left side of V neck. 29 (29, 29) sts.

To shape the neck

Row 1 (RS): Bind off 3 sts, work in patt to end. 26 sts.

Work 17 rows in eyelet patt, dec 1 st at neck edge on first 6 rows. 20 sts.

To shape the shoulder

Row 1 (WS): Bind off 6 sts, purl to end. 14 sts.

Rows 2: Work in patt.

Row 3: Bind off 7 sts, purl to end. 7 sts.

Row 4: Work in patt.

Bind off rem 7 sts.

To make the neckband

Block each piece. Join shoulder seams.

With RS facing, using size 3 (3.25mm) needles and yarn A, pick up and knit (see page 29) 3 sts from bound-off sts at R front neck, 5 sts along shaped edge of R front neck, 9 sts along straight edge of R front neck, 35 (37, 39) sts from back neck, 9 sts along straight edge of L front neck, 5 sts along shaped edge of L front neck, 3 sts from bound-off sts at L front neck. 69 (71, 73) sts.

Row 1 (WS): *P1, k1; rep from * to last st, p1.

Row 2: K1, *p1, k1; rep from * to end.

These 2 rows form K1 P1 rib patt. Work 1 more row in K1 P1 rib patt.

i like parties

Row 4 (eyelet row for knitted cord) [RS]:
Work 5 sts in K1 P1 rib patt, yo, k2tog, work in K1 P1 rib patt to last 7 sts, ssk, yo, work 5 sts in K1 P1 rib patt.

Work 7 more rows in K1 P1 rib patt, ending with WS row.
Drop yarn A. Join yarn B.
Knit 1 row then purl 1 row.

Next row (picot eyelet row) [RS]: K1, *yo, k2tog; rep from * to end.

Next row: Purl.

Cut yarn B. Rejoin yarn A and work 9 more rows in K1 P1 rib patt, ending with RS row. Leave all 69 (71, 73) sts on needle. Complete neckband after V neck edgings have been worked.

To make the edgings
Left side of neck
With RS facing, using size 5 (3.75mm) needles and yarn B, pick up and knit (see page 29) 7 sts along neckband side edge from picot eyelet row and then 30 (32, 34) sts along V neck edge. 37 (39, 41) sts.

Row 1 (WS): Purl.

Row 2 (picot eyelet row) [RS]: K1, *yo, k2tog; rep from * to end.

Next row: Purl.

Next row: Knit.

Fold over edging to WS. Sew edging in place as for shrug neckband (see page 35).

Right side of neck
With RS facing, using size 5 (3.75mm) needles and yarn B, pick up and knit (see page 29) 30 (32, 34) sts along V neck edge and 7 sts along neckband side edge to picot eyelet row. 37 (39, 41) sts.
Complete as for L side of neck.

To make the cord
Using size 2 (2.75mm) double-pointed needles and yarn A, make 2-st knit cord (see page 62) 31½ in./80cm long.

To complete the neckband
Fold over neckband to WS. Sew neckband in place as for shrug neckband (see page 35). Using yarn B, work almost invisible running sts through picot edging where it joins rib so that edging stands upright. Thread knit cord through neckband, with ends coming through eyelets at each end. Using yarn A, sew side edges of neckband into place on WS.

To make the armhole edgings
With RS facing, using size 5 (3.75mm) needles and yarn B, pick up and knit (see page 29) 5 sts along bound-off edge, 15 (17, 19) sts along shaped edge, 33 (33, 35) sts to shoulder seam, 34 (34, 36) sts to shaped edge, 15 (17, 19) sts along shaped edge, 5 sts along bound-off edge. 107 (111, 119) sts. Complete as for edging on L side of neck.

To make the knit pom-poms
Using size 3 (3.25mm) needles and yarn B, cast on 10 sts.

Rows 1 and 2: Knit. Cut yarn B. Join yarn A.

Row 3: Knit, leaving a long end. Thread tapestry needle with long end of yarn A and thread yarn through all 10 sts on knitting needle.

Row 4 (RS): Inc in every st. 20 sts.

Rows 5, 7, and 9: Purl.

Rows 6 and 8: Knit.

Rows 10: *K2tog; rep from * to end. 10 sts.

Cut yarn A, leaving a long end. Complete as for knit pom-poms for slipper socks (see page 57). Make 2.

To finish
Block picot points of edgings, omitting edging on neck rib. Join side seams. Attach knit pom-poms to cord.

Need an excuse to go out?
This skirt is your reason
to leave the house!

09 miniskirt

$\mathcal{C}$an you live without a knit miniskirt? We didn't think so. And this one has got the groove. Knit in plain stockinette stitch, this mini has a contrasting ribbed waistband and a front pleat. This pattern introduces you to knit hems, pleats, and herringbone casing . . . and it will improve your dancing (promise!).

To make the back

Using size 3 (3.25mm) needles and yarn A, cast on 145 (153, 161) sts.

Row 1 (RS): Knit.

Row 2: Purl. Rows 1 and 2 form St st.

Rows 3–5: Work 3 more rows in St st.

Row 6 (WS): Knit. This forms ridge for hem.

Rows 7–10: Work 4 rows in St st beg with knit row.

Row 11 (RS): Make the hem

The hem can either be sewn into place or knit on this row.

To make a sewn hem

01: WS facing: With sewing needle and thread in contrasting color, thread through every st along the Make the Hem row. Complete knitting.

02: Fold up hem to WS and sew into position, using thread as guide. Remove thread.

what you need:

tools:
pair size 3 (3.25mm) knitting needles
2 x size 3 (3.25mm) double-pointed knitting needles
size 6 (4mm) knitting needle
stitch markers
tapestry needle
straight pins
sewing needle & thread

materials:
yarn A: 3 (3, 4) x 1¾ oz./50g balls sport weight yarn (186 yd./170m per ball)
* we used ggh Merino soft, shade 65 in Bright Pink (100% merino wool)
yarn B: 2 (2, 2) x 1¾ oz./50g balls sport weight yarn (186 yd./170m per ball)
* we used ggh Merino soft, shade 15 in Black (100% merino wool)
½ yd./0.5m lining fabric (59 in./150cm w)
4 in./10cm long zipper to match yarn B
1 yd./1m elastic (1 in./2.5cm w) (optional)

gauge & measurements:
30 sts & 38 rows = 4 in./10cm
waistband: (small) 25½ in./70cm; (medium) 29½ in./75cm; (large) 31½ in./80cm/
length: (small) 12 in./30cm; (medium) 12 in./30cm; (large) 12 in./31cm

Casting on for a knit hem

01: Make slip knot (see page 13) and place onto LH needle. First st made.

02: Insert RH needle into front of slip knot. With index finger of R hand wrap yarn from right to left around point of RH needle and pull yarn toward you through slip knot to form another loop. Place new loop onto LH needle. Second st made.

03: Insert RH needle from front to back into st just made on LH needle. Wrap yarn from right to left around point of RH needle and pull yarn toward you through st to form another loop, then place new loop onto LH needle.

04: Repeat step 3 until required number of sts are on LH needle. Cast-on row will form loops to be picked up when making knit hem.

To make a knit hem

01: On the Make the Hem row, fold hem to WS.

02: Insert RH needle into first cast-on loop and lift onto LH needle. Knit tog first st on LH needle and cast-on loop.

03: Insert RH needle into next cast-on loop and lift onto LH needle. Knit tog next st on LH needle and cast-on loop. Cont across row to complete hem.

04: For pleat, purl together st on LH needle and cast-on loop as the 2 purl sts appear across row.

Rows 12–14: Work 3 rows in St st beg and end with purl row.

To make the side shaping

Beg with knit (RS) row, cont in St st dec 1 st at each end of the first and every foll 9th row until 129 (137, 145) sts rem.

Dec on knit (RS) rows as foll: K2, k2tog, knit to last 4 sts, ssk, k2.

Dec on purl (WS) rows as foll: P2, ssp, purl to last 2 sts, p2tog, p2.

Cont in St st without shaping until work measures 8 (8, 8¾) in./20 (20, 22) cm from hem ridge, ending with knit (RS) row. Cut yarn A.

To make the waistband

Join yarn B.

Row 1 (WS): Purl.

Row 2 (RS): *K2, p2; rep from * to last st, k1.

Row 3: P1, *k2, p2; rep from * to end. Rows 2 and 3 form K2 P2 rib patt. Cont in K2 P2 rib patt until waistband measures 2 in./5cm, ending with WS row.

Next row (dec row) [RS]: [K2, p2] 1 (1, 2) times, [k2, p2, k2, p2tog, k2, p2, k2, p2, k2, p2tog] 6 (3, 3) times, [k2, p2] 0 (2, 2) times, [k2, p2, k2, p2tog, k2, p2, k2, p2, k2, p2tog] 0 (3, 3) times, [k2, p2] 1 (1, 2) times, k1 (1, 1). 117 (125, 133) sts.

Next row (WS): P1 (1, 1), [k2, p2] 1 (1, 2) times, [k1, p2, k2, p2, k2, p2, k1, p2, k2, p2] 6 (3, 3) times, [k2, p2] 0 (2, 2) times, [k1, p2, k2, p2, k2, p2, k1, p2, k2, p2] 0 (3, 3) times, [k2, p2] 1 (1, 2) times.

Next row (RS): [K2, p2] 1 (1, 2) times, [k2, p2, k2, p1, k2, p2, k2, p2, k2, p1] 6 (3, 3) times, [k2, p2] 0 (2, 2) times, [k2, p2, k2, p1, k2, p2, k2, p2, k2, p1] 0 (3, 3) times, [k2, p2] 1 (1, 2) times, k1 (1, 1). Rep last 2 rows until waistband measures 3 in./7.5cm, ending with WS row.

Next row (dec row) [RS]: [K2, p2] 1 (1, 2) times, [k2, p2tog, k2, p1, k2, p2, k2, p2tog, k2, p1] 6 (3, 3) times, [k2, p2] 0 (2, 2) times, [k2, p2tog, k2, p1, k2, p2, k2, p2tog, k2, p1] 0 (3, 3) times, [k2, p2] 1 (1, 2) times, k1 (1, 1). 105 (113, 121) sts.

Next row (WS): P1 (1, 1), [k2, p2] 1 (1, 2) times, [k1, p2, k1, p2, k2, p2, k1, p2, k1, p2] 6 (3, 3) times, [k2, p2] 0 (2, 2) times, [k1, p2, k1, p2, k2, p2, k1, p2, k1, p2] 0 (3, 3) times, [k2, p2] 1 (1, 2) times.

Next row (RS): [K2, p2] 1(1, 2) times, [k2, p1, k2, p1, k2, p2, k2, p1, k2, p1] 6 (3, 3) times, [k2, p2] 0 (2, 2) times, [k2, p1, k2, p1, k2, p2, k2, p1, k2, p1] 0 (3, 3) times, [k2, p2] 1 (1, 2) times, k1 (1, 1). Rep last 2 rows until waistband measures 4 in./10cm, ending with WS row. Bind off in patt using size 6 (4mm) needle.

To make the front

Use a separate ball of yarn A for each side of front. Using size 3 (3.25mm) needles and yarn A, cast on 65 (69, 73) sts, with yarn B, cast on 47 sts, and with separate ball of yarn A, cast on 65 (69, 73) sts. 177 (185, 193) sts.

knitting with 2 colors

When **changing colors**, avoid making a hole as follows: with both yarns on WS, drop first yarn, pick up 2nd yarn and wrap it around first yarn before working next st.

Row 1 (RS): Using yarn A, k65 (69, 73), using yarn B, sl 1 wyif, k7, sl 1 wyib, k29, sl 1 wyib, k7, sl 1 wyif, using yarn A, k65 (69, 73).

Row 2: Using yarn A, p65 (69, 73), using yarn B, k1, p45, k1, using yarn A, p65 (69, 73). Rows 1 and 2 form St st with edges of front pleats.

Rows 3–5: Rep rows 1 and 2 once then row 1 once more.

Row 6 (WS): Knit. This forms ridge for hem.

Row 7 (RS): Using yarn A, k65 (69, 73), using yarn B, sl 1 wyib, k7, sl 1 wyif, k29, sl 1 wyif, k7, sl 1 wyib, using yarn A, k65 (69, 73).

Row 8 (WS): Using yarn A, p65 (69, 73), using yarn B, p8, k1, p29, k1, p8, using yarn A, p65 (69, 73).

Rows 9–10: Rep rows 7 and 8 once.

Row 11 (RS): Make hem (see pages 48–9).

Rows 12–14: Rep row 8 once then rows 7 and 8 once more.

To make the side shaping

Beg with a knit (RS) row, cont in St st with center pleat as established, dec 1 st at each end of first and every foll 9th row until 161 (169, 177) sts rem. Dec on knit (RS) rows as foll: K2, k2tog, work in patt to last 4 sts, ssk, k2.

Dec on purl (WS) rows as foll: P2, ssp, work in patt to last 2 sts, p2tog, p2.

Cont in St st without shaping until work measures 8 (8, 8¼) in./20 (20, 21) cm from ridge at the hem, ending with knit (RS) row. Cut yarns.

To form the pleat

Join yarn B and use across whole row.

Pleat row (WS):

01: P49 (53, 57), slip next 8 sts onto double-pointed needle, then slip next 8 sts onto 2nd double-pointed needle.

02: Twist needle holding second set of 8 sts so that WS sts are facing WS of first set of 8 sts and RS sts are facing RS of rem sts on LH needle.

03: With needle holding first set of 8 sts at the back, needle holding second set of 8 sts in middle, and LH needle at front, purl tog st from each needle onto RH needle, dropping all 3 sts (1 from each needle) when purl st is complete.

04: Cont to purl across rem 7 sts, 1 st from each of the 3 needles together to make 1 st on RH needle.

05: Now p15 sts from LH needle to RH needle.

06: Slip next 8 sts onto double-pointed needle and next 8 sts onto 2nd double-pointed needle.

07: Twist needle holding second set of 8 sts so that RS sts are facing RS of first set of 8 sts and WS sts are facing WS of rem sts on LH needle.

08: With needle holding first set of 8 sts at front, needle holding 2nd set of 8 sts in middle, and LH needle at back, purl tog first st from each needle onto RH needle, dropping all 3 sts (1 from each needle) when purl st is complete.

09: Cont to purl across rem 7 sts, 1 st from each of the 3 needles tog to make 1 st on RH needle.

10: Purl across rem 49 (53, 57) sts. 129 (137, 145) sts.

To make the waistband

Using yarn B, work as for back waistband.

To finish

Complete hem (see pages 48–9). Block each piece (see page 18) omitting ribbing and folding front pleat at slipped stitches.

To make the lining

01: Lay skirt back on piece of paper and pin, opening rib to get full width under waistband. Trace skirt back, marking points on either side where St st and ribbing meet. Remove skirt back from paper and draw a line joining the points you have marked.
02: Draw another line ½ in./1cm out from side seam lines and ¾ in./2cm out from hem.
03: Draw another line ½ in./1cm out from line marking joining points between St st and ribbing. Cut around these outer lines.
04: Lay paper on lining fabric and pin into place. Cut lining using paper patt as a guide. Remove paper. Fold paper in half from hem to waist and cut along fold. Insert piece of paper to widen skirt at center front by 4 in./10cm. Use this to cut out lining for skirt front. Sew side seams, making a ⅝ in./1.5cm seam.
05: Fold ½ in./1cm of bottom edge to WS of lining and sew into place. Fold up another ¾ in./2cm and sew with hemming sts. Fold over ½ in./1cm at top to WS of lining. Fold center front of lining to match knit pleat. Press.
Sew side seams, leaving top 4 in./10cm open at left side for zipper.

To make a herringbone casing (optional)

This holds the elastic flat at the waistband.
01: Using yarn B, secure yarn to bottom L 1¼ in./3cm from bound-off edge and on first k2 (as viewed from WS) of ribbing.
02: Bring yarn to top R, inserting needle from R to L through knitting at bound-off edge and on next knit st(s) (as viewed from WS) of ribbing.
03: Bring yarn to bottom R, again inserting needle from R to L through knitting 1¼ in./3cm from bound-off edge and on next knit st(s) (as viewed from WS) of ribbing. Cont working until completed. Fasten off securely.

To sew in the zipper

01: With RS of knitting faceup, place RS of zipper against WS of knitting. Pin in place, making sure that knitting does not overlap zipper teeth and that both sides of the knitting are evenly matched.
02: With RS faceup, sew zipper into position using backstitch, folding and stitching the top ends of zipper to WS. Slip stitch edges of zipper tape to knitting on WS.

Match side seams and center front and center back. Pin lining into position at beg of waistband and sew into place on first row of waistband. If used, measure the elastic for a comfortable fit and thread through herringbone casing.
Sew side edges of elastic to secure.

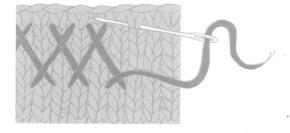

herringbone casing is worked from L-R

10 pom-pom hat

Do you dream of a hat that has style *and* keeps you warm on the frostiest winter morning? Then this is for you. Knit in seed and garter stitch, it is worked evenly up to the crown and then finished with a very easy shaping sequence. We've also added pom-poms. Just for fun.

To make the hat

Using size 6 (4mm) needles and yarn A, cast on 101 sts.
Row 1: *K1, p1; rep from * to last st, k1.
Rep row 1 forms seed st patt. Work 18 more rows in seed st. Hat should measure 2½ in./6cm from cast-on edge. Cut yarn A. Join yarn B.
Row 20 (RS): Knit.
Work 31 more rows in seed st. Hat should measure 6½ in./16cm from cast-on edge.
To shape the crown
Crown is worked in garter st (knit every row).
Row 1 (RS) and Row 2: Knit.
Row 3: *K23, k2tog; rep from * 3 times, k1. 97 sts.
Rows 4–8: Knit.
Row 9: *K10, k2tog; rep from * 7 times, k1. 89 sts.
Rows 10–14: Knit.
Row 15: *K9, k2tog; rep from * 7 times, k1. 81 sts.
Rows 16–20: Knit.
Row 21: *K8, k2tog; rep from * 7 times, k1. 73 sts.
Rows 22–26: Knit.
Row 27: *K7, k2tog; rep from * 7 times, k1. 65 sts.
Row 28: Knit.
Row 29: *K6, k2tog; rep from * 7 times, k1. 57 sts.
Row 30: Knit.
Row 31: *K5, k2tog; rep from * 7 times, k1. 49 sts.
Row 32: Knit.
Row 33: *K4, k2tog; rep from * 7 times, k1. 41 sts.
Row 34: Knit.
Row 35: *K3, k2tog; rep from * 7 times, k1. 33 sts.
Row 36: Knit.
Row 37: *K2, k2tog; rep from * 7 times, k1. 25 sts.
Row 38: Knit.
Row 39: *K1, k2tog; rep from * 7 times, k1. 17 sts.

what you need:

tools:
pair size 6 (4mm) knitting needles
tapestry needle

materials:
yarn A: 1 x 1¾ oz./50g ball thick DK/thin worsted weight yarn (118 yd./108m per ball)
* we used Rowan Summer Tweed, shade 527 in Acid Green (70% silk, 30% cotton)
yarn B: 2 x 1¾ oz./50g balls thick DK/thin worsted weight yarn (118 yd./108m per ball)
* we used Rowan Summer Tweed, shade 531 in Chocolate Brown (70% silk, 30% cotton)
stiff cardboard or plastic for pom-poms

gauge & measurements:
seed st: 19 sts & 32 rows = 4 in./10cm
circumference: 20½ in./52cm

Row 40: Knit.
Row 41: *K2tog; rep from * 7 times, k1. 9 sts.
Row 42: Knit.
Cut yarn and thread through tapestry needle. Use tapestry needle to thread yarn through 9 sts rem on needle. Remove needle from sts and pull to gather sts. Secure yarn.

To finish

Block (see page 18), omitting garter st shaping. Join back seam using invisible weave seam method (see page 18), reversing seam for 1½ in./4cm above cast-on edge for the cuff.
Make pom-poms
Using yarn A, make 2 x 1¼ in./ 3cm-diameter pom-poms and 1 x 1½ in./4cm-diameter pom-pom (see page 62). Sew along R side of hat.

11 slipper socks

$\mathcal{O}$h at last, slippers to celebrate in. Made from the top down in stockinette and garter stitch, these slipper socks knit up in a jiffy. Secure them at the ankle with a cute drawstring, scatter with sequins, and dance the night away, twinkle toes!

$\mathcal{T}o$ make the slipper socks

Using size 10.5 (7mm) needles and yarn A, cast on 27 (31) sts using method for knit hem (see pages 48–9).

Row 1 (RS): Knit.

Row 2: Purl.

Row 3: K1, *yo, k2tog; rep from * to end.

Row 4: Purl.

Row 5: Knit.

Row 6: Purl.

Drop yarn A. Join yarn B.

Row 7 – make picot hem (RS): Fold first 6 rows to WS. Insert RH needle into first cast-on loop and lift onto LH needle. Knit tog first st on LH needle and cast-on loop. Insert RH needle into next cast-on loop and lift onto LH needle. Knit tog next st on LH needle and cast-on loop. Cont across row until hem is complete.

Row 8: Purl.

Row 9: Knit.

Row 10: Purl.

Drop yarn B. Pick up yarn A.

Row 11 (RS): Knit.

Row 12: Purl.

Row 13: K1, *yo, k2tog; rep from * to end.

Row 14: Purl.

Cut yarn A. Pick up yarn B.

what you need:

tools:
pair each sizes 10 & 10.5 (6mm & 7mm) knitting needles
size 10.5 (7mm) circular needle or 1 spare size 10.5 (7mm) knitting needle
2 x size 10 (6mm) double-pointed knitting needles
tapestry needle
stitch holders

materials:
yarn A: 1 (2) x 1³/₄ oz./50g balls bulky weight yarn (71 yd./65m per ball)
* we used Debbie Bliss Cashmerino Chunky, shade 17005 in Bright Pink (55% merino wool, 33% microfiber, 12% cashmere)
yarn B: 3 (3) x 1³/₄ oz./50g balls bulky weight yarn (71 yd./65m per ball)
* we used Debbie Bliss Cashmerino Chunky, shade 17001 in Black (55% merino wool, 33% microfiber, 12% cashmere)
72 x ¹/₅ in./5mm-diameter black sequins

gauge & measurements:
St st: 14 sts & 22 rows = 4 in./10cm
foot length: 9¹/₂ in./24cm (10 in./25.5cm)

Row 15 – make fold (RS): Fold last 4 rows to WS. Insert RH needle into first yarn B loop on row 11 (color change) and lift onto LH needle. Knit tog first st on LH needle and yarn B loop. Insert RH needle into next yarn B loop on row 11 (color change) and lift onto LH needle. Knit tog next st on LH needle and yarn B loop. Cont across row until fold is complete.

Row 16: Purl.

Row 17: Knit.

Row 18: Purl.

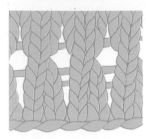

*picot hem
as knit*

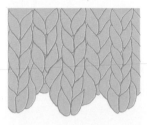

*completed
picot hem*

Change to size 10 (6mm) needles.
Row 1: *K1, p1; rep from * to last st, k1.
Row 2: P1, *k1, p1; rep from * to end. Rows 1 and 2 form K1 P1 rib patt. Cont in K1 P1 rib patt for 2 in./5cm, ending with row 1. From now on, WS of the first 18 rows will be RS of slipper sock. When slipper sock is completed, first 18 rows will fold over to outside (RS).
Change to size 10.5 (7mm) needles.
Row 1: Knit.
Row 2: Purl. Rows 1 and 2 form St st.
Cont in St st until slipper sock measures 8 in./20cm, ending with a purl (WS) row.
Next row (eyelet row) [RS]: K2, *yo, k2tog; rep from * to last st, k1.
Next row: Purl.

To divide for the instep
Row 1: K18 (21), turn and work on these 18 (21) sts. Leave rem 9 (10) sts on holder.
Row 2: P9 (11), turn and work on these 9 (11) sts for instep. Leave rem 9 (10) sts on holder.
Beg with knit row, work 30 (32) more rows in St st. Leave sts on needle. Cut yarn B.

To begin the foot
Using size 10.5 (7mm) circular needle, return 9 (10) sts left on first holder to needle. With RS faceup, rejoin yarn B, pick up and knit (see page 29) 21 (22) sts along side of instep, knit 9 (11) sts from needle at instep, pick up and knit 21 (22) sts along other side of instep, knit 9 (10) sts from 2nd holder. 69 (75) sts.
If using size 10.5 (7mm) straight needle, return the 9 (10) sts left on first holder to needle. With RS faceup, rejoin yarn B, pick up and knit (see page 29) 21 (22) sts along side of instep, knit 5 (6) sts from needle at instep, using 2nd size 10.5 (7mm) needle, knit rem 4 (5) sts from needle at instep, pick up and knit 21 (22) sts along other side of instep, knit 9 (10) sts from 2nd holder. 69 (75) sts.
Work back and forth on these 69 (75) sts. If using straight needles, change needles at same place on each row.
Next row (WS): Knit.
Work 8 (10) more rows in garter st (knit every row), ending with WS row.

To shape the foot
Row 1 (RS): K1, k2tog, k29 (32), ssk, k1, k2tog, k29 (32), ssk, k1. 65 (71) sts.
Rows 2, 4, 6, and 8 (WS): Knit.
Row 3 (RS): K1, k2tog, k27 (30), ssk, k1, k2tog, k27 (30), ssk, k1. 61 (67) sts.
Row 5 (RS): K1, k2tog, k25 (28), ssk, k1, k2tog, k25 (28), ssk, k1. 57 (63) sts.
Row 7 (RS): K1, k2tog, k23 (26), ssk, k1, k2tog, k23 (26), ssk, k1. 53 (59) sts.
Bind off knitwise.

To make the drawstring

Cord
Using size 10 (6mm) double-pointed needles and yarn A, make a 2-st knit cord (see page 62) 15¾ (17¾) in./40 (45) cm long (or length desired) for each slipper. Make 2.

Knit pom-poms
Using size 10.5 (7mm) needles and yarn B, cast on 7 sts.

Rows 1–2: Knit.

Cut yarn B. Join yarn A.

Row 3: Knit, leaving a long end. Thread tapestry needle with long end of yarn A and thread yarn through all 7 sts on needle.

Row 4 (RS): Inc in every st. 14 sts.

Row 5: Purl.

Row 6: Knit.

Row 7: Purl.

Row 8: *K2tog; rep from * to end. 7 sts.

Cut yarn A, leaving a long end.

Thread tapestry needle with long end of yarn A and thread yarn through all 7 sts on needle. Remove needle and pull thread tightly to gather sts. Secure yarn. Do not cut yarn but use to sew seam after yarn B is removed from bottom edge. Cut away yarn B from bottom edge. The yarn threaded through the sts on row 3 will hold the sts in place. Cut short lengths of yarn A and use to stuff the ball firmly. Pull end of yarn A at bottom of pom-pom to close and secure yarn end.
Make 4.

To finish

Block each slipper sock (see page 18). The points of the picot folds should point to the cast-on end of the sock. Do not block K1 P1 rib.

sew sequins onto top (St st) section of foot in diamond pattern

Sew sequins onto top (St st) section of the foot, randomly or in diamond pattern as illustrated above.

Join back and underfoot seams. Use invisible weave seam (see page 18) to join the back of foot. Thread cord through eyelets at ankle, with ends of cord at the back. Sew pom-pom onto each end of cord.

12 earmuffs

These are extra cute and super warm – and they are made in wonderful curly Astrakhan. Worked as a single piece, they are shaped by changing the length of the rows. Perfect for cold mornings and sledding down hills.

To make the earmuffs

Using size 7 (4.5mm) needles and yarn A, cast on 100 sts.

Row 1 (WS): Knit.

Cut yarn A. Join yarn B.

Rows 2–3: Knit.

Cut yarn B. Join yarn C.

Rows 4–5: Knit.

To shape the bottom half of the first earmuff

These are worked in short rows (see page 31).

Row 1 (RS): K29, turn.

Row 2: K8, turn.

Row 3: K10, turn.

Row 4: K12, turn.

Row 5: K14, turn.

Row 6: K15, turn.

Row 7: K16, turn.

Row 8: K18, turn.

To shape the bottom half of the second earmuff:

Row 9 (RS): K63 sts, turn.

Rows 10–16: Rep rows 2 to 8 as bottom half of first earmuff.

Row 17 (RS): K34 sts (to end of row).

Rows 18–23: Knit across all 100 sts.

To shape the top half of the first earmuff

Row 1 (WS): K34, turn.

Row 2: K18, turn.

Row 3: K16, turn.

Row 4: K15, turn.

Row 5: K14, turn.

Row 6: K12, turn.

Row 7: K10, turn.

Row 8 (RS): K8, turn.

what you need:

tools:
pair size 7 (4.5mm) knitting needles
tapestry needles

materials:
yarn A: 1 (1) x 1³/₄ oz./50g ball worsted weight yarn (76¹/₂ yd./70m per ball)
* we used ggh Big Easy, shade 014 in Bright Pink (100% cotton)
yarn B: 1 (1) x 1³/₄ oz./50g ball worsted weight yarn (76¹/₂ yd./70m per ball)
* we used ggh Big Easy, shade 001 in White (100% cotton)
yarn C: 1 (1) x 1³/₄ oz./50g ball worsted weight yarn (76¹/₂ yd./70m per ball)
* we used Debbie Bliss Cashmerino Astrakhan, shade 31004 in Chocolate Brown (60% merino wool, 30% microfiber, 10% cashmere)

gauge & measurements:
yarn C: 18 sts & 36 rows = 4 in./10cm
circumference: 22 in./56cm

To shape the top half of the second earmuff

Row 9 (WS): K63 sts, turn.

Rows 10–16: Rep rows 2 to 18 as top half of first earmuff.

Row 17 (WS): K29 sts (to end of row).

To make the top border

Row 1 (RS) and 2 (WS): Knit across all 100 sts.

Cut yarn C. Join yarn B.

Rows 3–4: Knit.

Cut yarn B. Join yarn A.

Rows 5–6: Knit.

Bind off purlwise (see page 17) (on RS).

To finish

Block (see page 18). Use invisible weave seam (see page 18) to join side edges.

pom-
poms

13

*P*om-poms – we *love* them! So simple to make and fabulous for using up little bits of yarn. Pin them on your socks, sew them to your picnic blanket, or as we have here, wear them around your neck and hang them from the doorframe. Best made while chatting with your friends.

To make the necklace

Using size 2 (2.75mm) double-pointed needles and yarn A, make a 2-st knit cord (see page 62) 30 in./75cm long or length required. Leave cast-on and bound-off ends of cord hanging. If you prefer, use a store-bought cord or ribbon of the same length.

Using yarn B, make 1 pom-pom 1½ in./4cm in diameter and 2 pom-poms 1¼ in./3cm in diameter (see page 62). Using yarn C, make 2 pom-poms 1¼ in./3cm in diameter.

Thread a tapestry needle that will pass through the bead holes with either end of cord or ribbon. Thread pom-poms onto cord in following order:
Bead
1¼ in./3cm-diameter pom-pom in yarn B
Bead
1¼ in./3cm-diameter pom-pom in yarn C
Bead
1½ in./4cm-diameter pom-pom in yarn B
Bead
1¼ in./3cm-diameter pom-pom in yarn C
Bead
1¼ in./3cm-diameter pom-pom in yarn B
Bead

Arrange so that 1½ in./4cm-diameter pom-pom is in center of cord. Sew ends of cord.

what you need:

tools:
2 x size 2 (2.75mm) double-pointed knitting needles
tapestry needle

materials:
yarn A: 1 x 1¾ oz./50g ball sport &/or light worsted weight yarn
* we used ggh Merino soft, shade 65 in Bright Pink (100% cotton)
yarn B: 1 x 1¾ oz./50g ball sport &/or light worsted weight yarn
* we used Rowan Summer Tweed, shade 527 in Acid Green (70% silk, 30% cotton)
yarn C: 1 x 1¾ oz./50g ball sport &/or light worsted weight yarn
* we used ggh Mystik, shade 097 in Dark Blue (54% cotton, 46% viscose)
30 in./75cm ribbon or cord (optional)
6 x ³⁄₈ in./10mm-diameter pink beads with large hole
stiff cardboard or plastic for pom-poms

measurements:
length of cord = 30 in./75cm (adjustable)

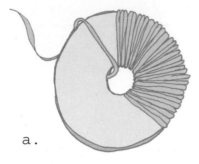

a.

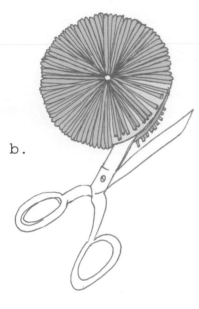

b.

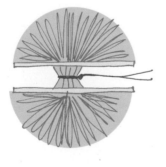

c.

To make a pom-pom

1   Draw a circle with diameter of pom-pom required on piece of stiff cardboard or plastic. Draw smaller circle in center of first circle, one-third to half the diameter of larger circle (a thicker yarn requires a larger inner circle). Cut out larger circle. Cut across cardboard/plastic into smaller circle and cut out smaller circle. One template made—it should look like a thick ring with a single cut from outer to inner edge. Make 2.

2   Place 2 circles together. Thread tapestry needle with yarn. Wind needle around and around the templates (*illus. a*) until templates are completely covered with yarn and hole is filled.

3   Cut yarn at outer edge (*illus. b*).

4   Pull 2 circles apart and wind another length of yarn between circles around central core of strands. Tie a tight knot (*illus. c*). Trim threads (or leave uncut if pom-pom will be sewn on). Remove template disks and fluff out pom-pom.

Note: If threading pom-pom, thread through center of pom-pom and pull cord through carefully, to avoid pulling pom-pom apart.

To make 2-st or 3-st knit cord

1   Using size 2 (2.75mm) double-pointed needles, cast on 2 (3) sts and knit them from LH needle to RH needle. Without turning needle, push sts to other end of RH needle.

2   Again, without turning needle, hold needle in LH ready to knit 2 (3) sts again. Yarn will be hanging at the L of sts. Bringing yarn behind sts, knit 2 (3) sts.

3   Repeat step 2 for desired length. A circular cord will be formed. Bind off.

To make the hanging

Using size 2 (2.75mm) double-pointed needles and yarn A, make a 3-st knit cord (see page 62) 61 in./155cm long or length required. The extra 2 in./5cm is to make the loop for hanging. Leave cast-on and bound-off ends hanging. If you prefer, use a store-bought cord or ribbon of the same length.

Using yarns B–E, make pom-poms (see page 62) in a mix of sizes. We used a total of 20–25 pom-poms per hanging in 4 sizes—¾ in./2cm, 1¼ in./3cm, 2 in./5cm- and 3 in./8cm-diameter pom-poms.

Thread a tapestry needle with either end of cord (or ribbon). Thread pom-poms onto cord in a random order or following illustration (see page 61) and arrange decoratively. Fold over top 2 in./5cm of cord and sew end into place to form a loop for hanging. Sew cast-on and bound-off ends of cord.

what you need:

tools:
2 x size 2 (2.75mm) double-pointed
knitting needles
tapestry needle

materials:
yarn A: 1 x 1¾ oz./50g ball sport &/or
light worsted weight yarn of your choice
yarn B—E: 5 yarns of your choice
** thicker yarn makes larger pom-poms
*** avoid yarns that fray or unravel easily

2 yd./2m ribbon or cord (optional)
stiff cardboard or plastic for pom-poms

measurements:
length of hanging = 59 in./155cm
(adjustable)

Many thanks to: Catie Ziller for her original idea
& for making things nicer with croissants; Pauline
Hornsby for her perfect knitting; Kathy Steer &
Sarah Rock for (more) hard work & advice; Ben &
Ruth for the photos; Matt for the camera; & . . .

...to stuart, grace, & poppy miller with love...

xxx xxx xxx xxx

your turn on the computer now, Stu xxx

First published in the United States in 2007 by
Watson-Guptill Publications
a division of VNU Business Media, Inc.
770 Broadway, New York, NY 10003
www.watsonguptill.com

Library of Congress Control Number: 2006936848

ISBN-10: 0-8230-9982-2
ISBN-13: 978-0-8230-9982-5

First published in France by Marabout
(Hachette Livre) in 2006
© 2006 Marabout (Hachette Livre)

Printed in China

First printing, 2007

1 2 3 4 5 6 7 8 / 14 13 12 11 10 09 08 07

The quantities of yarn are based upon average requirements and are therefore approximate.
Yarns & advice supplied by LOOP, 41 Cross St, London, N1 2BB, www.loop.gb.com